Welcome to Healing
By Amber K and Azrael Arynn K

When faced with illness or injury, people throughout the ages and all over the world have asked goddesses and gods of medicine, health, and healing for their help. You can do the same.

Whether you think of ancient deities as psychological archetypes, powerful spirit beings, different aspects of a single Creator, or something else... doesn't matter. Whatever their nature, they have been essential to our species since the dawn of humanity, and working with them affects our emotions and thoughts, and thus even our biochemistry.

In addition to gods and goddesses you've heard of—Isis and Brigit, Apollo and Hygieia—many less well known are waiting for you: Babalú Ayé, Ebisu, Heka, Nehalennia, Tawaret, and many more. Think of these as hidden treasures now come to light, spiritual resources waiting centuries or millennia for your call, to answer your need.

This book doesn't offer easy answers or instant miracles. We don't even provide canned prayers to the various divinities we describe. We do, however, describe many ways to form a relationship with a healing deity or Divine Array, how to honor and work with them, and how you can help manifest health on the physical plane. This path requires your serious effort.

"The gods help those who help themselves." Be prepared to do some work. Cooperate with your physicians and healers to help your body here on the material plane, then open yourself to the radiant love of your allies in Spirit.

More books by Amber K

Moonrise: Welcome to Dianic Wicca
    (Re-Formed Congregation of the Goddess, 1992)
Pagan Kids' Activity Book
    (Amber K, 2000)
The Goddess Coloring Book
    (Amber K, 2000)
True Magick: A Beginner's Guide
    (15th Anniversary edition, Llewellyn, 2005)
CovenCraft: Witchcraft for Three or More
    (Out of print, coming soon from Amber K)

More books by Amber K and Azrael Arynn K

Heart of Tarot: A Gestalt Approach
    (Out of print, coming soon from Amber K and Azrael Arynn K)
Candlemas: Feast of Flames
    (Llewellyn, 2003)
RitualCraft: Creating Rites for Transformation and Celebration
    (Llewellyn, 2006; Winner of COVR Awards
    for Best Wiccan/Pagan Book 2006 and Book of the Year 2006)
How to Become a Witch: the Path of Nature, Spirit, and Magick
    (Llewellyn, 2010)
True Wand Magick: Desire, Will, and Focus
    (with CreateSpace, 2016)
Amber and Azrael also contributed chapters to
Exploring the Pagan Path: Wisdom from the Elders
    (New Page Books, 2005)

This book is dedicated to Worldwalker and Coyote Bridge, who know a thing or six (thousand) about healing: body, mind, emotions, and spirit. With love and admiration from Amber and Azrael

Healing with the Gods and Goddesses

Divine Allies on Your Journey to Health

Amber K and Azrael Arynn K

Healing with the Gods and Goddesses: Divine Allies on Your Journey to Health © 2018 Amber K and Azrael Arynn K. All rights reserved. No part of this book may be reproduced in any manner whatsoever, including Internet usage, without written permission from Amber K or Azrael Arynn K, except in the case of brief quotations embodied in critical reviews.

FIRST EDITION
February 2018

Book design by Azrael Arynn K
Cover design by Amber K
Cover photograph by foxaon1987/Shutterstock 116758246
Cover image of Hygieia by Natalia Barashkova/Shutterstock 776942575
Original interior illustrations by Amber K

ISBN 978-1984004390

Disclaimer:
Any Internet references contained in this work are current at publication time, but the authors cannot guarantee that a specific location will continue to be maintained.

This book does not provide medical advice.

The contents of this book, such as text, graphics, images, information quoted from other sources, and other material contained in the book are for informational purposes only.
   The content is not intended to be a substitute for professional medical advice, diagnosis, or treatment. Always seek the advice of your physician or other qualified health provider with any questions you may have regarding a medical condition. Never disregard professional medical advice or delay in seeking it because of something you have read in this book!
   If you think you may have a medical emergency, call your doctor or 911 immediately.
   You should always consult with your healthcare professional prior to using any medication, nutritional, herbal or homeopathic product or before beginning any exercise or diet program or starting any treatment for a health issue.
   Any suggestions regarding the spiritual, emotional, or other support of the healing process are strictly the authors' own personal views made in their own personal capacity, and are not intended as a substitute for appropriate medical care or advice from a healthcare professional. Reliance on any information provided by the authors is solely at your own risk. The authors make no guarantee or warranty with respect to any information provided or techniques discussed, and are not responsible for any damages arising from misuse of material included in this book.

Published with CreateSpace
Printed in the United States of America

Contents

Introduction vii

SECTION ONE Partnering with the Divine 1

Chapter 1 How the Gods and Goddesses Can Help You on Your Journey to Health 1

Chapter 2 Choosing a Deity and Building a Relationship 15

Chapter 3 Ritual with Your Deity 31

Chapter 4 More Spiritual Techniques 49

Chapter 5 Acting in Accord 67

SECTION TWO The Goddesses and Gods of Healing 83

Part 1 Featured Gods and Goddesses 85

Airmed: herbs, battle wounds, resurrection 86
Anahita: sacred sexuality, childbirth, sacred water 87
Angitia: herbs, magick, snakebite 88
Apollo: sun, healing, plagues, wounds 89
Artemis/Diana: fertility, childbirth, mental health, protector of women and children 91
Asclepius: medicine, healing, rejuvenation 93
Babalú-Ayé: infectious diseases, epidemics 96
Beiwe: fertility, mental and emotional health, SAD 98
Bona Dea: fertility, healing, regeneration, protector of abused women, herbal medicines 99
Borvo: healing waters, medicinal potions 101
Brigit: fertility, childbirth, eyes, leprosy, healing wells and springs, magick, healer of animals 102
Carna: physical and spiritual health, internal organs, digestion, well-being 104
Chinese Deities of Health and Healing 105
Chiron: general healing, teacher of healers 107
Dhanvantari: Ayurvedic medicine, blood disorders, herbs ... 109
Dian Cécht: medicine, battle wounds 110
Ebisu: children's health, workplace injuries, bones 112

Eileithyia: fertility, childbirth, midwives, children 114
Eir: medical skill, childbirth, children, epidemics 115
Endovelicus: health, safety, healing waters, dreams 116
Erinle: patron of LGBT, herbs, bodily fluids 117
Erzulie/Erzulie Mapiangue: health, healing, sexuality, gay men,
    magick/deals with pain of childbirth, protector of the
    unborn and newborn 118
Eshmun: healing, health, children, survivors of sexual abuse
    120
Fufluns: health, growth of all things, good cheer 121
Grannus: hot healing waters, diagnosis, the sun, sunburn,
    sunstroke 122
Gula: The Great Physician, creation, illness and good health,
    medicine, healing, fever, inflammation, fatigue, magick,
    and dreams 123
Haumea: fertility, childbirth, death and rebirth 125
Heka: health, wellness, medicine, magick, the life force 127
Herakles: men's health, and their strength, fertility, and
    sexuality 129
Hygieia: health, especially cleanliness, hygiene, sanitation,
    prevention of illness and infection, preventive
    medicine, mental health, herbs 130
Isis: sexuality, fertility, motherhood, children's illnesses,
    healing, magick, protector of the dead, reincarnation
    and rebirth, snakebite, massive injury 132
Ixchel: sexual relations, women's fertility, childbirth, midwifery,
    medicine, general healing 135
Kumugwe: healing waters, general healing 137
Kupalo/Kupala: cleansing water, health, longevity, herbs,
    mental and emotional health, infection 139
Kwan Yin: fertility, childbirth, health, healing, purification;
    compassion for grief, suffering, and despair 140
Mama Cocha: healing water, healing, health, nutrition, stress
    and mental health 143
Mami Wata: healing, health, fertility, sex, water 144
Mati Syra Zemlya: health, healing, fertility, sperm, childbirth,
    midwifery, protection from illness and epidemics 146

Menrva: health, medicine, mental and emotional health 148
Nehalennia: healing, fertility, emotional healing 150
Ninhursag: herbs, fertility, midwifery, newborns, motherhood 152
Nodens: healing, childbirth, injuries sustained on the sea or while hunting, war wounds, emotional health, healer of dogs 154
Pajau Yan: health, healing, menstruation, immortality, peaceful death, resurrection 156
Sekhmet: healing, medicine, surgery, bone-setting, sunburn, sunstroke 157
Shaushka: sexuality, androgyny, bisexuality, health, healing 159
Sirona: healing of illness and injury, healing springs 161
Sitala: cholera, dysentery, all infectious diseases, cools fevers, emotional health 162
Tawaret: fertility, pregnancy, childbirth, newborns, nursing mothers, children, death and rebirth 164
Uretsete and Naotste: health, healing, teacher 166
Vejovis: protection from plagues and natural disasters 167
Part 2 Additional Goddesses and Gods 169

Part 3 Planetary and Zodiac Gods and Goddesses 195

SECTION THREE Appendices 199

Appendix A Cross-Reference by Specialty 201

Appendix B Cross-Reference by Region and Culture 207

Appendix C Healing Modalities 235

Appendix D The Middle Pillar for Healing 239

Appendix E Symbols 243

Appendix F Reading List 251

Introduction

If you are ill or injured and want to enhance your healing process with the help of Spirit, in this case, the ancient goddesses and gods from cultures around the world, this book is for you.

If you are a healer, a nurse or physician or health professional of any kind, this book is also for you.... if you believe that healing involves the mind, emotions, and spirit interacting with the body.

However, this is no recipe book of miracles; if it were, we could simply list a bunch of relevant deities and offer some canned prayers and rituals, implying that if miracles are asked for in the proper manner, they will be granted. We do not believe that, and this is not that sort of book.

When we speak of working with the gods and goddesses of healing, we mean much more than simply praying to divine entities for miraculous intervention to fix us. The nature of deity and the many ways we can work with it, in all its aspects, are the subjects of the first few chapters, presented so you can understand what you are doing and approach the techniques in a creative and personalized way, a way that really works for you.

We do not mean to imply that a spiritual approach to healing is sufficient. Our belief is that "The gods help those who help themselves." This means that if you want to heal, you will need to take practical action for self-care and follow the guidance of health and medical professionals who know more than you do about the material side of healing.

To assume that there are strictly spiritual answers to all challenges would be to ignore the reality that we live in physical bodies on a material plane of existence. If the gods expect anything of us, maybe they expect that we will be smart enough to know that, and to handle the mundane aspects of healing like eating right, visiting our healers or doctors, taking our pills, and giving up stupid addictions that tend to kill us over time.

By all means, use the techniques suggested in this book. Take a spiritual approach to your health needs, and work the problem mentally, emotionally, and energetically as well. But do not expect that to be enough. It is not.

So, here's the disclaimer: the authors do not claim that following the techniques suggested in this book will heal you, at least not by themselves. The activities in this book are not a replacement for competent health and medical care by trained and licensed professionals. The activities in this book can only enhance that treatment, not replace it.

In writing this book, we did a lot of research into gods, goddesses, and other spirit beings important to various cultures around the world, and throughout history. We would not expect that all of our research is perfectly accurate, especially when dealing with the beliefs and deities of other cultures, some of them from civilizations long dead. If you, the reader, have strong evidence that we have made any error in characterizing these deities, please contact us with your insights and information so that we may correct future editions. Thank you!

In our own lives, we have called upon many of these goddesses and gods for help in dealing with our own health challenges, including cancer, diabetes, clinical depression, and bipolar disorder. We are extremely grateful to our medical teams and alternative healers for their care and guidance, and at the same time we feel certain that working with our special dieties has made a difference; at this moment, anyway, we are alive, happy, and productive. Blessings to all who have journeyed with us to this place.

And blessings to you, dear readers. We hope this book helps you in your healing journey, to alleviate your pain and the physical challenges you face. We wish for you a long, healthy, and joyous life... and if any part of that is not to be in this lifetime, we hope that you will find and create a far better reality when you return again to this world. Much love to each of you.

Blessed be,
Amber K and Azrael Arynn K
February 2018

Ardantane
P.O. Box 307
Jemez Springs, New Mexico 87025

SECTION ONE
Partnering with the Divine

Chapter 1
How the Gods and Goddesses Can Help You on Your Journey to Health

On the nature of the Divine

Let's start with this: who are the goddesses and gods?

If you talk to a Christian, they may say there is one God who created everything, and is all-powerful, all-knowing, and infinitely good....

Or is actually three gods in one (Father, Son, and Holy Spirit), can't know everything because he created us with free will, and allows evil to flourish in the world...

Or if you are Hindu, there are many gods, most of whom are aspects or avatars of others...

Or perhaps you believe that all the gods and goddesses are different faces of one Supreme Being: "All goddesses are one Goddess; all gods are one God; Goddess and God are One."

Or if you are a "hard polytheist," maybe you believe that every deity is a separate and individual divine Person...

And—one of our personal favorites—perhaps the gods began as "what if" imaginary or theoretical beings, but evolved into more as people started to believe in them, and then invested mental energy in them.

Chapter 1

Imagine that 50,000 years ago, Morg says to his buddy (as a storm rages and they cower under a tree):

> "What if the thunder is made by a mighty being with a huge club, pounding on the mountain peaks?"
>
> His friend Gronk replies, "That could make sense. If he's real, he must be very strong. Do you think he could help us bag a mammoth on the next hunt?"
>
> Morg: "Sure, if he wanted to. Let's offer him some tasty meat, and ask. Bort could ask, he knows lots of words and can even make songs. Bort could write a song to Thunder."
>
> Gronk: "Yes! We'll all sing a song to Thunder, and broil him some meat. He will smell it, and come to help us!"

Just suppose that the thoughts, prayers, hymns, and energies of millions of people, over centuries or millennia, could energize and animate a thought-form... such as the idea of a god. The prototypical entity might become more powerful, more complex, more *real* as human energy and desire flowed into it.

Deities could be our human forebears, beloved chiefs or mighty warriors or powerful shamans, who got promoted to godhood; or psychological constructs (imaginary friends on a grand scale); or inventions of con artist priests who saw religion as a profitable scam; or technologically advanced aliens from the planet Noodfizz who wowed our ancestors with pretty blue beads and shiny gadgets. Unless you have a strong faith in a particular theology, you may never be sure.

How fortunate, then, that we don't have to know who they are, in order for them to be helpful to us. You might know very little about your usual car mechanic (can you be certain he's not from the planet Noodfizz?), but he can still change your oil and maybe find that weird groaning ungga-ungga noise your car makes when you turn left. You don't really understand electricity, but it still runs your lava lamp and your "Hello Kitty" alarm clock. You don't have to understand the nature of divinity for the gods to help you.

So, how can the goddesses and gods actually help?

It's all a matter of perspective

Yes, the healing deities are known for their strength in the areas of health, medicine, herbs, etc., but they are not *only* healers, any more than your human healing partners (doctors, acupuncturists, herbalists, nutritionists, etc.) go through life just working their healing specialty. Your human partners have other interests: they may be gardeners, have pets, cook for pleasure as well as necessity, collect rocks, go camping, or know everything there is to know about that blue Amazonian butterfly.

The gods are similarly flexible and multi-faceted, so they bring all of their knowledge and wisdom, skills and magicks to aid you in healing. While this book is primarily about those gods and goddesses most known for their healing abilities, every god or goddess has a unique perspective, and that's why you may need to consult other deities—not necessarily those famous for healing—for more help.

In addition to looking at healing from the viewpoints of the various goddesses and gods, you can look at your healing process

Chapter 1

from the perspective of different aspects of your life. We have been using a tool we call the Life Compass for a few years, and have found that it offers insight into how the different parts of your life are doing. We sit down once a week and have what we call our "Summit," which includes everything from paying the bills to deciding who we want to send thank-you notes to this week, to looking at our lives in terms of the eight points of the compass and its center—the realm of Spirit. The nine parts of the compass are shown in the diagram below.

The Life Compass

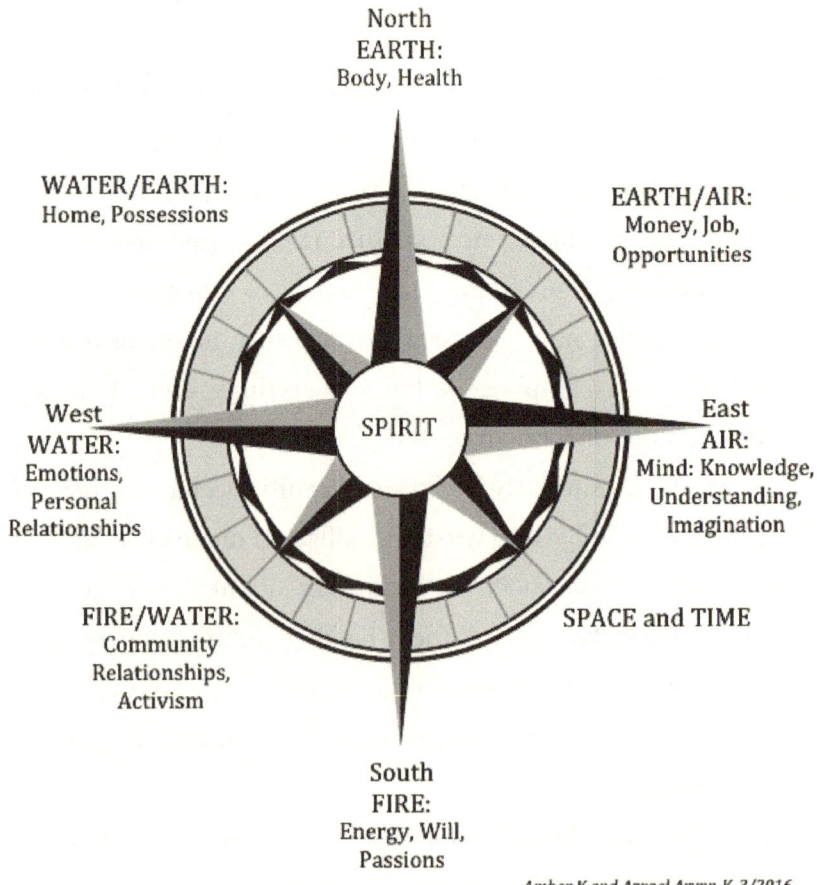

North
EARTH:
Body, Health

WATER/EARTH:
Home, Possessions

EARTH/AIR:
Money, Job,
Opportunities

West
WATER:
Emotions,
Personal
Relationships

SPIRIT

East
AIR:
Mind: Knowledge,
Understanding,
Imagination

FIRE/WATER:
Community
Relationships,
Activism

SPACE and TIME

South
FIRE:
Energy, Will,
Passions

--Amber K and Azrael Arynn K, 3/2016

All of these areas in your life can affect your health, or be impacted by your health. Every one of them can be aided by developing a connection to Deity. In the next section, we will cover them all in relation to deities who specialize in healing—and those who do not, but who can assist nonetheless.

Spirit

A rich spiritual life is bound to help your healing process. Working with Deity or deities reminds you of your connection with Spirit, which is always there, whether consciously or not.

One possibility is that gods and goddesses are powerful beings, sentient beings, who can choose to work "miracles" when you pray to them, just because you asked. Anything is possible, and how could you disprove it? If it is true, then it's worth communicating with them and to enlist their impressive powers to heal yourself or a loved one. We prefer to think of our communications with deity as "working with" them, rather than "praying to" them. This gives a more give-and-take aspect to the relationship, and empowers us as co-creators with them, rather than subservient beings in supplication to greater ones.

Mind, Imagination, Knowledge

If you trust psychology more than mythology, and understand deities more as archetypes, then—hey, still useful! Archetypes represent something real in the human psyche, and healing archetypes are a mirror for our own healing abilities. They reinforce the understanding that you can heal yourself, and can help you find and activate your own healing power. Indeed, in a sense all healing is self-healing (though this is not to diminish the help that medical professionals and healers can give you).

A deity can also be a mental focal point for your healing. The more focused we are on a task, the more time and thought and energy we put into it, the more likely we are to succeed. If the task at hand is to heal yourself, then every time you notice your shrine to Isis, or touch the Apollo talisman you made, or glance in a mirror and see yourself dressed in Brigit's red and white, then your thoughts will return to self-healing. This continual refocusing of your mind counteracts the natural tendency to escape an unpleasant or scary situation, to try not to think about it. Most of the time, running away is not useful.

With meditation and thought, your mind has a tremendous impact on your body and your health. When you call on one of the healing deities, your thoughts become aligned with their energies, and that can reflect itself in your body. For instance, if you enlist the aid of Māri for chicken pox, you are aligning your energies with her curative powers, and that can be reflected in a lessening of your symptoms—as long as you are supporting this on the physical plane (called Acting in Accord, see Chapter 5), and avoid doing anything counter-productive.

Getting to know the healing deities will help you gain knowledge about healing lore, ancient and modern. For example, the Celtic goddess Airmed can help you learn about herbs, Wang Wei (Chinese) helps you learn about acupuncture, and Dhavantari (Hindu) about Ayurvedic medicine. Glispa (Navajo), brought the Blessing Way ceremony to her people, and can help you discover how magic and ritual can help you heal.

Space and Time

Nuit exemplifies another benefit of having divine helpers: the gods and goddesses provide a different perspective on your life and issues, whether they relate to your health or anything else. Some, like Nuit, help you see the big picture; as the goddess of the heavens, she sees the very big picture—her perspective is enormous. She can help you understand the big questions: "What is my life all about? How does this injury or illness fit into the way I live, who I am, what I want? What am I doing right, and what must I change to become the person I want to be?" "How can I use this space and time of illness (or injury) to learn?"

Sometimes the gods just want us to slow down, give ourselves some space or time that we are unwilling to give ourselves. Perhaps you have experienced the truism that you *do* have time to slow down—you have to when you are sick or injured. Everything else becomes secondary, and you discover that it is possible to say "no" to that one commitment that you thought was imperative.... You also find that you *do* have space in your house for that piece of exercise equipment that the doctor ordered after your heart attack.... Perhaps Hestia, goddess of the hearth and home, can help you place that equipment where you will use it, so it becomes a part of your everyday living. Think about your priorities in terms of Maslow's hierarchy, in which your physical health and safety is the foundation for all else. If you "don't have time" to take care of your health first, the gods will make you make time, and then they will be there to guide you as you re-prioritize your life.

Chapter 1

Energy and Passion

Energy is everywhere. Everything is energy. All states of physical being, from debilitating illness to peak health are states of energy. All things in Nature are energy, and the gods and goddesses are no exception. As wielders of energy, they can aid in any energetic issues you may have. As an energy-wielder yourself, you can use your energy, and the energy around you, to call upon the deities to use theirs, and the energy goes around and around, building higher and higher until you are at peak health. Do you suffer from chronic fatigue? Ask a high-energy deity for help, like Shakti the sacred dancer, Ganesha who removes obstacles, Ares the god of battle, Pan who enlivens all nature, or Apollo the bright sun god.

You can also act in accord (see more about this in Chapter 5): if you're not up to wild, ecstatic dance with Shakti, at least move gently in her name, or walk for a while—any bit of movement will help almost any healing. Do you get out into the sun for at least 20 minutes a day? The sun (Apollo) can infuse you with energy (and increasing your vitamin D intake helps in many ways, too!). And try going without sunglasses, to absorb the full spectrum of light. (Did you know that South American tribespeople had no knowledge of cataracts until after Westerners introduced sunglasses to them?) Our eyes and bodies are designed through millions of years of evolution (no sunglasses back then!) to absorb sunlight, our main source of radiant energy. Use it.

What are your passions, and how can the gods help you create better health through following your passions, or so that you have energy to follow your passions? For instance, if your passion is that big blue Amazonian butterfly, you might call on Nehalennia.

She is a goddess of healing and travel, plenty, horticulture (butterflies pollinate flowers), and the harvest (your desired harvest is good health). If your dream is to go to the Amazon and photograph that blue butterfly in its natural habitat, Nehalennia could help heal you, so you could then make that journey. She might encourage you to spend a bit more time outdoors in fresh air, admiring and being healed by Nature, as well.

Passionate interests, beliefs, or goals ignite energy, and focused energy can heal.

Community Relationships and Social Activism

Sometimes it can be difficult to see how community relationships could affect your health. But just think, when was the last time the news "depressed you?" And how often does that happen? That kind of depression can build and feed on itself, wearing down your immune system. The body and mind ARE connected.

One thing you can do to alleviate this phenomenon is to get involved. If you are ill, write a letter to your Senator or Congresswoman. Donate to politicians and causes that support your views and beliefs. Taking action is one of the best ways to support your immune system and your emotional health. Helping others has been shown to have an extraordinary effect on overall happiness, emotional health, and even physical vitality.

At the very least, goddesses and gods can serve as role models who inspire us to be and do our best at the business of life; this includes maintaining our health and working to heal ourselves and others. If that's setting your sights too high, then we always have saints or superheroes as exemplars of what we can aspire to.

Chapter 1

Emotions and Personal Relationships

Emotions and personal relationships often go hand in hand. Other people can support you, or they can "tear you down," if you let them.

If you need emotional support or healing, you can get some of that from your chosen deity. Remember the Charge of the Goddess: "For My law is love unto all beings. By naught but love may I be known... I am the Mother of all things and My love is poured upon the Earth." Your divine companion will love you unconditionally, and show you how to be stronger emotionally and more loving in turn to others. Some deities help you see how to handle tough times, and the dark emotions that accompany them, like Inanna, the Sumerian goddess who entered the realm of death and suffered horribly to understand its Mystery. Sometimes it helps just to pour out your pain and fear and anger to Kwan Yin, or any other deity who provides a caring ear.

When we are sick or hurting, it is so easy to fall into a pit of depression and negative thinking. If you let them, the gods can keep your mind off your immediate complaints and on something higher: your life's purpose, your service to others, or your legacy. The Bodhisattvas (like Kwan Yin) will help you focus on the needs of others; they are evolved souls who had the choice to go on to Nirvana but chose to reincarnate for more lifetimes in order to be of service to others.

Once you make a genuine connection with your chosen deity, and start to experience him or her as an actual Person rather than a mythic figure, you will start to feel a warm, strong sense of companionship. Sure, your family and friends are there for you;

but they have other responsibilities to take care of, and maybe they have their own fears and worries about your situation that are not always comfortable for you. But a goddess or god who is also your friend can be there for you 24/7, and won't feed your fears with their own. Azrael once said, referring to the Egyptian sky goddess who is her healing companion, "Nuit is always there... She's got my back."

You have heard that older people who have regular interaction with dogs or cats are healthier and live longer than those who don't. And people in committed relationships are healthier and live longer than those who are single. If you are single and don't have a pet (or even if you are married and have two dogs), develop a relationship with a goddess or god, someone who will always be there with you, wherever you go. Allow the relationship to deepen, and it will nurture you; you will find yourself not only happier, but healthier.

if personal relationship challenges are impacting your health, you might call any divine couple (Shiva and Shakti, Frey and Freya) or deities who work in groups: the Greek Muses, or the healing family of Asclepius. Ask them: "How do you do that? How do you create and maintain a loving relationship, or work harmoniously as a team or group?"

Home and Possessions

Hertha is a Germanic goddess of the hearth and home. She can lead you to wonder, "How does my home contribute to, impact, or harm my health and healing? Do I need a HEPA air filter to alleviate my asthma, or should I move my bedroom to the guestroom on the south side for more sunlight? Do I need to look into green cleaning products and decrease my intake of household toxins? Do I need to dedicate a space in my home for exercise, and perhaps get a stationary bike or treadmill? How else could my home and possessions be affecting my health?"

Body and Health

When your problems are physical, of course you will want to work with the healing deities—but also any divine being who can help with your body image and your relationship with your body. If you have issues about being overweight, perhaps you could talk to Ho Ti, Ganesha, or Gaia, some very chunky deities who like themselves just fine. If you don't like your face, you might discuss your feelings with Tlitcaplitana, a goddess with a very large nose. If you have a handicap, talk to Hephaestus, the lame smith god. Very few deities have stereotypically perfect bodies and faces, and yet they are powerful and amazing divine beings.

Most of this book is about Body and Health, so we won't go into it more here.

Money, Job, and Opportunities

If you have financial issues related to your health and medical care, ask Lakshmi or another prosperity goddess to help with money, insurance, and so forth. Mercury or Hermes can also help with communications and paperwork.

Is your job in jeopardy because of health problems? Ask Sarasvati or Mercury to give you eloquence as you enlist the help of your boss and colleagues. If you lose your job unjustly due to illness or injury, ask Themis, the goddess of justice, to help you get it back or get compensation.

Ask the gods to help you discover hidden opportunities: is there a silver lining to this cloud? How does your illness or injury open new doors? Is the experience strengthening your attitude, mind, and coping skills? Could disability or unemployment benefits help you transition to a new career that would actually be more rewarding? What opportunities could this illness or injury be leading to?

Conclusion

You will want to work with a god or goddess who has strength and skill in healing, but you may go beyond this select company of deities and reach out to any divine personage who has the resources you need. Remember that the one you try first may not be responsive; the gods have their own missions, and they may also recognize that they are not a good fit for you in the work at hand. Try other possibilities, and you will receive a sign when you find the right one. Consider also that a goddess or god that you have not even thought about may choose to work with you; be open and alert to signals from unexpected directions. Such a communication may appear as a dream, an unusual occurrence involving a god's symbol, or "accidentally" coming across a deity's name, image, or myth in a book, online, or in conversation, or all of these in a single week! It's time to choose—or be chosen!

Chapter 2
Choosing a Deity and Building a Relationship

So, you've got your illness or injury. Now to find who can help. The many divine pantheons are like a very large family with many branches, and you can't really know all of them very well. However, they all know each other, and any deity from any pantheon may be willing to help any family member—you.

Choosing—or being Chosen?

You don't always have to make a choice. Often deity chooses you. A healing god or goddess may choose you according to whatever afflicts you. For example, if your eyes are bothering you, Brigit or Caolainn may have a message for you or want to work with you.

However, don't be surprised if you are tapped by a deity who seems to have little connection with health or healing. Divine beings can turn their powers to whatever they wish, and if a goddess has a particular interest in you, she may decide to help you heal. In addition, the causes of health problems are not always simple or obvious; the special domain of an unexpected deity may be relevant to your ailment.

Chapter 2

How do you know if a deity chooses you? Sometimes, as you read the gods' stories, or look at their images in art, you will simply feel an instant, strong attraction—a connection that has no obvious explanation. Perhaps you worshipped that deity in a former incarnation, or perhaps you just have an intuitive sense that this one is the one you need in your life right now. Trust your feelings, and explore further.

Occasionally a god or goddess who wants to connect with you will send a symbolic sign or message. It might be dramatic—a huge owl flies toward you as you take an evening walk, and you wonder if Athena has sent her messenger. The message may be more subtle—you step outside and notice vividly that the sunlight is warm on your skin and feels wonderful, like a benediction. Perhaps a sun god or goddess, Apollo or Amaterasu, is speaking to you.

Or maybe the name and image of a particular deity starts popping up repeatedly. Maybe you haven't thought of Bastet in years, then a friend names her cat after that goddess, and you see a statue of her in an ad for an Egyptian display at the museum, and a "stray" cat starts hanging around your home, and you go to a party where the host's three cats are all over you.

Pay attention. Follow up with meditation and communication, through divination or dreams. You will sense whether that goddess or god wants to become an ally.

But often no deity reaches out, and it is up to you to find a likely candidate and initiate the contact yourself. So, start researching. This book is a good beginning. In Appendix A, we've got the healing gods and goddesses of Section Two sorted into a table by their healing specialties—areas of the body and specific types of diseases. Start there. You have a broken bone? Sekhmet is an obvious possibility. Heart trouble? You can explore Carna/Cardea, or Mercury or a sun deity (astrologically, Mercury and the sun rule the heart). Surgery scheduled? Talk to Anubis, Miach, or Sekhmet. Dental problems? Consider Aibheaog or Hesy-Ra, among others.

Once you find one or more who address your problem, take time to meditate with each one. Ask what they are willing to do for you, and what if anything they want in return. Feel their energy, and whether it meshes with yours. Do you connect? If not, thank them, give them a small offering for their time, and move on to the next one.

It's all about mutual benefit and harmonious cooperation. Who feels right and is willing to work with you?

Getting to know your chosen deity

Over time you can develop a unique personal relationship with a goddess or god. This relationship will deepen your connection with your own divinity and the divinity in others. All spiritual paths offer resources (holy books, clergy, temples) or techniques (ritual, prayer, song, behaviors) to help adherents connect with the divine. However, the monotheistic churches promote that connection with only one aspect or face of the sacred (such as Allah), or a very few (Yahweh, Jesus, and the Holy Spirit). If you are reading this book, you have expanded the possibilities to include thousands of aspects: all the goddesses and gods of every human culture throughout history.

Once you've chosen (or been chosen by) your healing deity,

building a relationship with that divine personage will run along similar channels no matter who it is. The goal is to build an open, trusting relationship between the healer and the patient, or, even better, between two partners with the same aim.

Creating a relationship can begin in many ways. When you make a new human friend, you want to get to know them through a variety of activities: conversation, playing sports or games together, going on walks, working on projects, traveling, and so forth. If you only interact in one way—at work, or being on the same soccer team—you won't learn much about that person; there will be little depth to your relationship, or mutual understanding.

So, get to know your goddess or god from a variety of angles. Try several of the following approaches; some will work great, some not so well, depending on your skills and interests, and the personality of the god or goddess. As communication improves between you, you can ask your divine ally what they suggest.

- Read a book or books about your deity; if your goddess or god has no books written entirely about them, you'll need to look at encyclopedias of mythology and dig out the pertinent bits.
- Research your deity on the Internet; don't be surprised if you find many websites borrowing from one another, or conversely if you discover bloggers who have very different perspectives on your deity. That's natural.
- Create a journal or scrapbook about your deity; the first will have your personal observations and experiences, and the second will contain information and images that you have found in books and on the Internet.

- Have a conversation with your deity. How do you do that? It's much like prayer, except that you listen more than you talk, and hopefully you're not always asking for stuff. Work at it until you can easily distinguish the voice of divinity from your own self-talk.

- Read the myths about your deity; learn their titles, family relationships, and the stories about them that are so deep and meaningful that they have survived for hundreds of generations.

- Reenact a traditional myth of your deity, as sacred theater, with you in the role of your god or goddess.

- Write a new myth, story, or play about your deity, and tell it or perform it. Or do this with a small group of friends; you'll have really good discussions, and gain a lot of insight into the different ways your deity can be understood.

- Find statues or images of your deity; both as they are portrayed in their traditional culture, and as modern artists envision them. (Some of the modern god-and-goddess art is very striking and beautiful.)

- Create a painting or sculpture of your deity. If you don't have those skills, then try a collage. Cut out lots of colorful pictures from old magazines. Each should remind you of your deity, because of the subject matter, colors, the feelings the pictures evoke, or whatever. Arrange and paste them on a sheet of cardboard, perhaps within a large outline of your deity that you have drawn or traced. Meditate on the resulting art.

Chapter 2

- Create an altar or shrine for your deity. This could be in the form of a small table with a few significant objects on it... or one level of a bookshelf... or a drawer that keeps your goodies private until you slide it open... or a garden dedicated to your deity... or a flat stone at the base of your favorite tree... or even a grove of trees, with altar items that you bring out for rituals, or natural items that stay outdoors.
- Make a small offering at your shrine or altar; using their favorite foods and beverages, or music, or incense. Books may tell you the traditional offerings for this divinity, or you can ask during a meditation, dream, or conversation.
- Meditate on your deity, or visit her or him on a shamanic journey. If you have no experience with shamanism, someone in your community may know a practitioner they can recommend to guide you on your journey.
- Write a poem about your deity. No, it doesn't have to be a masterpiece. It doesn't even have to rhyme. It just has to express something important about your god or goddess. Try haikus if you've never written poetry. (A haiku is a short evocative poem, usually in three lines with seventeen or fewer syllables. A common form has 5 syllables, then 7, then 5 again.) Here's an example:

    Darkest night, path lost;
    Torchlight blooms, now Hekate
    Guides me to new life.

- Write and perform an invocation to your goddess or god. An invocation is a prayer or verbal appeal, calling upon a deity or spirit to be present and give aid. Often it is spoken at the beginning of a religious ritual or public ceremony. Here is an example:

  > Lady Brigit, goddess of inspiration, smithcraft, and healing, I call to you. Come to me from your green hills and holy wells, touch me with the gentle power of your healing hands, restore me to health and strength that I may walk with you in the sunlit high places, serving you and the Old Gods for the rest of my days. Dear Brigit, be welcome in this sacred circle.

- Write a letter to your deity. Think of it as a first letter to a new pen pal; introduce yourself, explain why you're writing, and what you hope for from the relationship. You may want to engage in regular correspondence.

- Find or make jewelry, or a talisman, focused on your god or goddess. You may be able to find a ready-made piece of jewelry online or at a conference or festival where Pagan silversmiths and artisans sell their wares. However, you can also make an inexpensive talisman from wood, bakeable clay, or hobby-shop craft materials. Use symbols and colors associated with your deity, perhaps an image of your divine partner decoupaged onto a wooden disk.

- Do dreamwork centered on your deity. Lucid dreaming techniques are taught in many books and online.

A simple approach is to put pen and paper by your bedside, drink a cup of mugwort tea, then meditate on an image of your god or goddess just before you go to sleep, while asking him or her to communicate with you as you dream. The moment you wake up, write down any visions or phrases you remember.

- Teach a class (or just lead a discussion) about your deity to your spiritual group. If you are not currently part of a group, then you might offer to teach a workshop at a Pagan festival, or to a study group or CUUPS chapter (Covenant of Unitarian Universalist Pagans), or offer a class at the public library. If you are doing this as part of your healing and spiritual growth, it is probably not appropriate to charge for the program.

- Get some body painting or henna done, in a theme your god or goddess would enjoy; or even get a tattoo, if you feel you have a lifetime commitment to that deity.

- Dance with or for your goddess or god. This can be a simple, freeform expression of love and gratitude done in the privacy of your home or yard; but if you are a serious dancer, it could also be a performance at any event that seems appropriate.

- Find, or create, a chant or song for your deity. Few deities have dedicated music that you can easily find. However, you can take an existing chant and think of new words for it, such as this example to the tune of the "Isis, Astarte" chant:

CLImbing the LYFjaberg, EIR I COME to you;
HERE I SEEK your POWers of... HEALing!

- Of course, if you are a musician and songwriter, you can create something entirely new. Whether you share it at a public event or keep it private is up to you.
- Aspect your deity, when and if you are ready. Aspecting—also called "assuming the god-form," or "drawing down the moon" if a lunar deity is involved—is an advanced spiritual practice. It means that you offer your body as a vessel for the divine being to incarnate on this plane. It is a powerful and life-changing experience, but should not be attempted until you have had training from experienced priests or priestesses.
- Create a costume of your deity, or a priest/ess outfit as clergy to that god or goddess. A costume can be used in ritual, especially if you are aspecting that deity. A clergy outfit announces to the community and the world that you have a spiritual vocation, and that one particular aspect of deity commands your devotion. If you have no flair for fashion or costume design, you probably know someone who does.
- Find one or more symbols associated with your deity (colors, gems, animals, objects, etc.) and ask yourself how you might include them in a a craft project that could become the centerpiece of a shrine or altar.
- Create an astral temple. You can create a temple dedicated to your goddess or god in your mind, and

place it on an astral plane where only you can find it. Because it is not built with bricks and mortar, you can make it as extensive, complex, and beautiful as you wish. Visit it in trance or during meditation whenever you want to connect with your divine partner.

- Create a ritual for your deity that is satisfying to all the senses: visual, auditory, and kinesthetic. If others are present, you may share your art, invocation, poetry, song or chant, a story or myth, a mystery play, or guided meditation.
- Hold a weekend retreat focused on your god or goddess (or a class of deities that includes yours: healing water goddesses, sun deities, etc.). If you have friends who would be open to such an experience, get them involved.

Serving deity: What do the gods require from us?

We hope you have been clear what you need from your divine partner. Yet energy must flow both ways, to reach a balance. So, ask yourself: what does this divine being want from me?

Service to your god or goddess strengthens your personal connection, but also makes you a better human being and hopefully serves your local community when you become an agent of the divine, and personify the values they represent.

You might consider pledging to perform a particular task or project in their honor, or vowing a year's service to your goddess or god, or even dedicating yourself as a priestess or priest of that deity if the bond between you has become deep and precious.

There are many paths of service, in addition to some of the possibilities mentioned in the list above:

- Do the work of the god or goddess in your career or as a serious, satisfying avocation (teaching, environmental stewardship, healing, etc.). This can be a lifelong endeavor or a very specific project that you will complete.
- Live a life that honors your particular goddess or god, by exemplifying the virtues they best represent.
- Deep aspect (deity assumption) in community ritual, in order to share wisdom or prophesy to others.
- Teach about your god or goddess, with particular emphasis on the wisdom and understanding they have to share with modern audiences.

Whatever form of service you choose, you may want to launch it with a ritual in which you clearly express what you choose to do, and seal your intention with solemn oaths.

Creating a Divine Array as a healing team

We mentioned earlier that you may choose, or be chosen by, more than one deity. We call this group of deities a Divine Array. The Divine Array you assemble for help with your healing may include only healing deities, or it may also include one or two whose specialty is different but who are on your team anyway, bringing their talents to your aid. For instance, Athena is not usually considered a healing goddess (except in the context of healing communities), but perhaps she is your favorite goddess, and will bring her clear-eyed wisdom to the table to help you see the big picture: what this illness or injury means to your life, and to those around you.

We recommend working with a Divine Array of three to five deities. More gets a bit complicated to track, just as having more than three to five doctors can get overwhelming. With fewer gods and goddesses, you can get to know each one well, and each will have a prominent place on the team.

However, we suggest working with one deity to start. Get to know that god or goddess really well, using the techniques from earlier in this chapter. Work with them for a while before adding another to your Divine Array (unless you are already very familiar with several others).

Conclusion

Human friendships tend to grow gradually over time, often in fits and starts. An initial thrill of discovery as you realize you've found a new friend may shift to a period when the relationship is still novel and shiny, and New Friend can do no wrong: flaws and irksome habits are invisible. Later there may be stretches of time when you take your friend for granted, or when you become irritated by the foibles you once thought charming. After a trip or event together, you might feel a surge of fondness and a deepening of the bond between you. Or there might be arguments and even temporary estrangements, followed by making up and renewing the friendship so that it is stronger than ever.

With working partnerships, as when you are doing a project on the job together, the focus is on the task at hand rather than exploring a relationship. Familiarity, respect, and even friendship may grow over time, but usually with less drama and fewer fluctuations in your feelings about each other.

Be prepared for both kinds of relationship when you work with a deity. You are doing a job together—getting you healthy—but it's not only that. A kind of intimacy develops, because you are working together on very personal stuff, not just a work thing; your well-being and perhaps your survival are at stake. Also, much of the interaction happens in your mind, heart, and spirit; your divine partner knows you better than any human friend ever could.

Unfortunately, your *human* friends and co-workers may move to another place, or be left behind as you change employers. But your goddess or god will always be only a thought away from you; once a deep connection has been made, they are with you for a lifetime. Even if you forget about them for long stretches, or discover new deity-aspects who answer your changing needs, or even if you change religions... your sacred partner will always be within you, waiting to help you, waiting for your call.

Chapter 2

Questions to Ask Your Goddess or God

1. What do you look like when you appear to humans?
2. Do you shapeshift into other favored appearances? What are they?
3. Do you have special skills or strengths other than the ones usually attributed to you in books and websites?
4. What part of the year is sacred to you?
5. Do the phases of the moon affect my interaction with you? If so, how?
6. What animals are special to you, and why?
7. What colors do you particularly enjoy?
8. Is there a tree, flower, or other plant that is sacred to you?
9. Do you have tools or objects that are associated with your work or nature?
10. What was your native country like, when you first became known to humanity?
11. What kinds of places are especially sacred to you? (mountains, deserts, waterfalls, seashores, forests, etc.)
12. If I were to make a pilgrimage to visit you, where would I go?
13. Do you have one or more holy days, or festivals?
14. How would you like your holy days to be celebrated?
15. What kind of offerings do you prefer?
16. What elements would you like to see in a ritual performed in your honor?
17. What do you want your devotees to do in the world? What kind of service do you desire from them?

18. Is there an organization, service, or charity that reflects or exemplifies your energy and purpose?
19. Who is under your special guidance or protection?
20. What are some qualities of character that you represent?
21. How would my life be different if I were more like you?
22. What does our world look like through your eyes?
23. What does human society look like through your eyes?
24. Do you prefer worship, mutual cooperation, or another form of interaction with humans?
25. If I were to share my experience of you with my friends or colleagues, how would you like to be presented?
26. Do you have a message for humanity?
27. Do you have a message specifically for me?

Chapter 3
Ritual with Your Deity

Ritual is one of your best tools for connecting with your god or goddess, and enlisting their power to support your healing.

So what is "ritual," when it's not just some repeated activity like brushing your teeth? In our book *RitualCraft* we define it as "an organized process that is sometimes prescribed or repeated, but can be experimental and—dare we hope—creative. It takes place outside of ordinary reality. It is physical, mental, and emotional. It involves at least two levels of mind, changes consciousness, and moves energy. It is focused on achieving a goal, which may be spiritual, as in honoring Deity or connecting with it... You could also call it theater for Younger Self, ephemeral multimedia art on two planes of reality...." and so on.[1]

To put it more simply, it is a series of actions that prepares you for making a change in yourself or the world, followed by raising and directing power for that change, followed by some more actions to get you back to the ordinary world. Ritual works in the realms of mind, emotions, and energy, so the results are often felt internally, and are not directly visible to others.

---

[1] *RitualCraft: Creating Rites for Transformation and Celebration*, by Amber K and Azrael Arynn K, Llewellyn Publications, 2006, p. 5.

Chapter 3

Types of Ritual

Ritual can be divided into several big categories, any of which can be focused on healing:

SEASONAL RITUALS (sabbats) help us celebrate the changing seasons. In most modern Pagan traditions, eight sabbats are celebrated, drawn primarily from Celtic culture:

- YULE (winter solstice, about December 21st): The longest night of the year, the rebirth of the sun, gift-giving, the World Tree.
- IMBOLG (about February 1st): Returning light, the earliest signs of spring, as well as cleansing, consecration, and the goddess Brigit.
- OSTARA (spring equinox, about March 21st): Spring, fertility, renewal, rebirth, and the goddess Eostre.
- BELTANE (about May 1st): Life, sexuality, creation, and the god Bel.
- LITHA (summer solstice, about June 21st): The longest day of the year, the sun at the height of its power, sun gods and goddesses.
- LUGHNASSAD (about August 1st): The grain harvest, fruition, and the god Lugh.
- MABON (fall equinox, about September 21st): The fruit and vegetable harvest, abundance, giving thanks, appreciating all that you have.
- SAMHAIN (October 31st): The meat harvest, remembering and honoring ancestors and those who have passed recently, the end/beginning of the Celtic year.

These occasions can attune you to the strong energy currents of the season, so that you may use those energy currents to heal. For example, in the early spring sabbat of Imbolg, cleansing and purification are appropriate goals, while at Beltane you can absorb the energy of rebirth, renewal, and growth for restoring your strength after illness. At a sabbat later in the year, such as Mabon or Samhain you might release negative thoughts and feelings that stress you and inhibit your health.

MOON RITUALS (esbats) allow the same thing, except that you are using the energies of particular lunar phases instead of seasonal currents. From New Moon to Full, energies for healing and growth are building. At the Full Moon when lunar power peaks, draw in its energy to yourself as you visualize yourself in a state of perfect wellness. As the moon wanes and diminishes in size, focus on releasing illness and weakness.

RITES OF PASSAGE mark important transitions in life: those most often recognized are birth, baby naming and blessing, puberty, coming of age/adulthood, school graduations, marriage, retirement, elder status, and funerals/memorial services. However, you can also design rites of passage to mark important stages in recovery of your health, such as giving up addictions, returning to full mobility after physical therapy, or finishing chemo and radiation and being cancer-free.

SPECIAL RITUALS FOR A PARTICULAR PURPOSE, such as healing rituals that draw upon the powers of your chosen gods and goddesses. These can be as simple or complex as you like, and may call upon one or more deities.

Chapter 3

The Benefits of Ritual

What is it about ritual that can help you in your healing?

Ritual gets your mind totally focused on the issue at hand: healing yourself.

Ritual can require a major effort to design, set up, and perform; this tells yourself and the gods that you are serious.

Ritual positively affects your emotions, helping you feel empowered and hopeful.

Ritual can be (should be) performed in a cast circle, which concentrates and focuses the power you raise, and keeps negative or distracting energies out.

Ritual takes you out of your body's immediate aches and pains, and puts you in touch (aligns you with) a wider reality, the "Realms of the Mighty Ones" (inside the circle), away from the "World of Humanity" or mundane reality (outside the circle). "Mighty Ones" refers to our ancestors, who are thought to be exalted in power and wisdom in the next life, and in a broader sense the term can include deities and other spirits.

Calling the Quarters in ritual reminds you that authentic healing is holistic, and engages mind (Air), energy (Fire), emotions (Water), body (Earth), and Spirit toward your goal.

Ritual serves as a beacon to deities and spirits, calling them to aid you.

Ritual leads you into a zone where you are balanced, healthy, and empowered (especially if you aspect or "draw down" a deity). You can "anchor" this state and train yourself to return to it at will.

Using music in ritual engages both the left and right sides of your brain, both analytical and holistic, which increases your likelihood of success. You can choose a "theme song" or particular chant for your healing; use it in the ritual and often afterwards.

Ritual performed with a group multiplies the energy you have to work with, assuming the participants are attuned ("in sync") with one another and focused on the same goal.

Sabbats and esbats can attune you to the energy currents of the season and the moon, so that you may use those energies to boost your healing.

Rites of Passage allow you to redefine yourself, leaving your old persona (and limitations including illness, disability, and bad habits that harmed your health) behind, to embrace a new, stronger, and healthier you as part of your new role and responsibilities.

Rituals to do with your chosen gods and goddesses not only focus their special powers on your healing needs, but deepen and strengthen your relationship with their energy so the benefits of the energy flow are ongoing.

Steps of Ritual

Most religions use ceremony or ritual as a way to create closer bonds with Deity/Spirit, and of course the forms vary a great deal. Here we will briefly review the basic steps of ritual within a fairly characteristic modern Pagan tradition, and the reason for each step. Feel free to adapt this outline to your own spiritual path. For more detailed information on creating ritual, see our book *RitualCraft*, mentioned earlier.

1. Preparation: You will want to prepare yourself, the space where you will perform the rite, and any people joining

you. Prepare yourself by grounding, centering, meditation, a cleansing bath, possibly fasting, and putting on whatever special clothing (such as robes or jewelry) makes the event feel special. Prepare the space by creating a shrine or altar, and arranging any lighting or decoration you wish. Prepare other participants by discussing the reason for the ritual beforehand, explaining their roles, and perhaps practicing songs or chants. Choose a time and day that seem appropriate, perhaps based on astrology, the phase of the moon, or a table of planetary hours.

2. Welcoming Participants: If others are helping, greet them as they arrive and express your gratitude for their support.

3. Pre-ritual Activity: This may simply be a review of the ritual that is about to begin, or possibly a briefing or teaching on the condition you plan to heal, and the god and/or goddess that will be invoked.

4. Attunement: In a group, connect with the others with a chant, a short guided meditation, or an exercise to ground and center. If you are working alone, you can still ground, center, and attune to any Element or spirit ally you wish.

5. Asperging: This is a ritual purification of yourself and the space. It can be done with a smudge stick (burning sage or sweetgrass), incense, salt and sprinkled water, a broom, or any method you choose. Sweep away all negativity and distractions, leaving the space clean and welcoming for your deity.

6. Casting the Circle: Create sacred space by drawing a circle around you and your altar, and the other participants, clockwise with a sword, athame, wand, or staff. This makes

a boundary to hold in energy and keep out the mundane world, and negative or inquisitive spirits.

7. Calling the Quarters: Face east (the direction of the Element of Air), south (Fire), west (Water), and north (Earth), and invite the spirit of each Element to be present and support your work. You may also wish to invite the energies of Above, Below, and Center.

8. Invoking Deity: Invite your chosen god or goddess (or one of each), to be present and lend their power to your healing ritual. You may also wish to call on the Ancestors.

9. Statement of Purpose: Clearly state your purpose aloud, whether or not you have human friends present and participating. If only for clarity in your own mind, and for the benefit of spirit beings present, state what you are doing and the outcome you intend.

10. Core Activity: At the center of your ritual is a special activity that directly addresses your healing needs. Many possibilities are outlined in the section that follows this outline of ritual.

11. "Cakes and Wine": If you have raised power, help yourself ground afterwards by having a bit of food and beverage. This might be the traditional "cakes and wine/ale," but could be a little bread and pure water, or even dark chocolate and champagne. If you haven't raised a lot of energy and don't need grounding, you can offer the victuals in honor of the cooperating spirits, or skip this step.

12. Farewell to Deity: Thank the attending god(s) or goddess(es), and either say farewell for the moment, or ask them to stay with you until your healing is complete.

13. Farewell to the Quarters: Say your thanks and farewells to the Elemental spirits of Earth, Water, Fire and Air, and Above, Below, and Center, if you invited them in.
14. Opening the Circle: Draw (counterclockwise) the energy outlining the circle's boundary into your athame or other tool, or allow it to sink into the Earth. Say any closing words that are appropriate to your tradition. We often use "The circle is open, but never broken. Merry meet, and merry part, and merry meet again. Blessed be."
15. Social Time: If other people have participated with you, you may want to spend a little time enjoying refreshments together, sharing good thoughts and feelings about the ritual, and discussing other ways they can support your healing.
16. Cleanup: You will want to tidy up and put away your ritual tools, etc. Or do it tomorrow.
17. Act in Accord: See Chapter 5.

Note that songs or chants may be interspersed throughout the ritual, to raise power, focus your mind, relax and soothe, or mark transitions from one activity to the next. Recorded background music is one option, but be courageous in using your own voice or musical instruments as well—whether or not you can sing or play really well. This is not a talent contest, and all that really counts is energy and intent.

Ritual Core Activities

Ritual is the vessel for a magickal working that helps draw allies, focus your purpose, and contain the energy. But at the heart of each ritual is the core, the focal point, the spell. Here are some activities that can comprise that core.

- Invoke your goddess or god. Let yourself enter a light trance, and imagine your whole being, Element by Element: Air (your mind), Fire (your energy body), Water (your emotions), Earth (your physical body), and Spirit. Gently explore each one, noting any part that seems weak or injured. With your breath, draw energy from the earth, sky, moon, or other favorite source, and bathe that weak or injured part of you with cleansing, healing power.
- Do the same, but this time visualize your body, part by part (feet, ankles, calves, etc.) from the ground up... if any part needs help, again draw energy and channel it into that part.
- Do the same, but this time see each system of your body (skeletal, muscular, circulatory, nervous, endocrine, digestive, etc.); breathe and draw energy into that system.
- Do the same, but this time visualize each major chakra (root, sexual, energy, heart, throat, third eye, crown); again draw energy, this time into any chakra that seems weak, dim, or discolored, until it becomes bright and strong and clear.
- Fill your favorite cup, chalice, or goblet with pure water (or you can use an infusion of a healing herb, or envision a healing color filling the water). Bless it in the name of the deity you are working with. Charge the

water with healing energy—you can use breathing, chanting, singing, playing a musical instrument, or even dancing. Slowly drink it, feeling its cleansing and healing energy flowing into you and through you. Take your time. When you have finished, give thanks to your god or goddess.

- With your wand, draw a healing symbol in the air. (It could be a reiki symbol, or the Rod of Aesclepius, or another symbol from Appendix D in this book. A friend of ours uses an image of a web charged with lightning! Draw the symbol into your solar plexus, then to the afflicted area. If you don't know a healing symbol that seems appropriate, ask your goddess or god to provide you one in a meditation, vision, or dream... or simply use your favorite image of that deity.

- Do a guided meditation in which you travel to your deity's temple and receive healing directly from her or him. You can write and record the meditation yourself, then play it back; or have a friend read it aloud for you.

- Dance out your illness, or visualize yourself dancing if you cannot move well. You can also drum out your illness. Be sure you have a place to send it; for example, deep into the earth, where mother Gaia can transform the energy into something positive.

- Release your pain or illness into a stone (not one you particularly treasure). Go to a private place some distance from your neighborhood and workplace, call upon your deity's help, and cast the stone far away from you. The negative energy will soak into the earth and be transformed.

- Write this question on a piece of parchment: "What does this illness or injury have to teach me?" Burn the parchment, and watch the smoke and your message float upward to the astral planes. Ask your god or goddess to give you an answer. Your reply may come in a dream or during meditation.
- Use this adaptation of the traditional Nine-Knot Spell. Find a length of cord of a color you associate with healing, and at each line tie a knot in the cord. If you can raise power by having one of the other participants drumming as you speak, so much the better.

   By knot of one, the cure's begun;
   By knot of two, I will come through;
   By knot of three, recovery;
   By knot of four, my power restore;
   By knot of five, my strength revive;
   By knot of six, the ailment fix'd;
   By knot of seven, the help of heaven;
   By knot of eight, regenerate;
   By knot of nine, good health is mine!

- Perform an adaptation of the Middle Pillar exercise, using healing deities rather than the original Hebrew names of God. See Appendix D.
- Aspecting, also known as "assuming the god-form," or "drawing down the moon" when done with a lunar deity, is a sacred experience in which you offer your

body as a vessel for a god or goddess to inhabit for a brief time—in this case, your divine healing ally. The experience can certainly boost your healing efforts; indeed, it can be life-changing. However, it is not something to attempt unless a) you have been trained by an experienced Craft elder, and b) you have a seasoned helper present to support you before, during, and after the event. Aspecting is too complex to cover in this book, but you should be aware of the option in case you have the training, or have resources in your community to learn it.

A Ritual to Support Healing of Breast Cancer

Here is an example of a ritual to support the healing of breast cancer.

Gather the following items:
- A pink, rose, or light green altar cloth
- An image of your chosen goddess (perhaps Aphrodite, since the breasts are often important to a woman's sexual identity; or Artemis of Ephesus, the many-breasted mother of life; or another goddess of life and health)
- Two pink candles
- Rose incense
- A pink rose in a bud vase
- A polished, smallish piece of rose quartz (2" diameter), smooth and fairly flat if possible; or a rose quartz necklace.

1. Asperge (cleanse the space) with water that you know to be pure, using the rose to sprinkle yourself and the ritual space. Do a simple circle-casting, such as the following:

   "I conjure thee, O circle of power, to be a boundary between the world of humanity and the realms of the Mighty Ones, a guardian and a protection, to preserve and contain the power I shall raise within; wherefore, do I bless and consecrate thee."

2. Cleanse the rose quartz with salt and water. Consecrate it, using language along these lines:

   "I consecrate thee, o creature of magick, in the name of the Lady Artemis of Ephesus, to be a vessel for healing energy, that you shall carry the power I place within you and feed it gently to me over time, that my breast(s) shall be whole and healthy again. By the power of the Goddess who is life and love, so mote it be!"

3. Now charge the stone or pendant. You can breathe power into it, or raise energy by chanting, dancing, drumming, etc., then pour it into the stone. Remember to use energy that you channel from outside and through you, not your own reserves. If it is a polished, flattish stone, carry it in your bra. If a pendant or necklace, simply wear it until the cancer is completely gone (removing it only momentarily for medical exams or radiation treatment).

4. Afterward, ground yourself and eat something.

5. Thank the goddess, open the circle, and act in accord, cooperating with your medical team and other healers.

6. When the cancer is gone, cleanse the rose quartz and gift it to someone else who is going through the same experience.

More on Rites of Passage

As mentioned earlier, rites of passage allow you to redefine yourself, leave behind your old persona, and embrace a new role and responsibilities; they are commonly performed on occasions such as adulthood (coming-of-age), marriage, and religious initiations. However, they can be done at any point when you are ready for a major change in your life. Such as healing.

In the ritual (and after) you will release your old self. Perhaps this will include your illness or disability; but maybe releasing something else seems more achievable at this point. Bad habits that harmed your health in the first place. Useless anger at your condition. A belief that you are incapable or doomed, that you cannot do good things or experience happiness. In extreme cases, when you are sure that physical death is imminent, maybe all you can release is fear and despair; and yet, wouldn't that be a monumental accomplishment!

Decide who you are ready to become, define your new self, and hold a ritual to mark this life-changing transition to:
Person-Who-Amazingly-Heals-Myself-And-Others... or
Person-Who-Loves-My-Body-And-Takes–Care-Of-My-Health... or
Person-Of-Unlimited-Possibilities-Who-Rides-A-Magnificent-Wheelchair ... or
Person-Who-Releases-Addiction-And-Embraces-Life; or even,
Person-Who-Leaves-A-Beautiful-Legacy-And-Meets-Death-With-Dignity-and-Grace.

Then you embrace this new and different you, with the help of your loved ones and your community. Be clear with them exactly what you need to help you make this transition. Do not hesitate to ask, because you are doing them a favor: you are providing the opportunity to give something meaningful to one they love (you), and to feel good about themselves by doing so.

A successful rite of passage includes several key parts. Here's a checklist of things that should happen:

DEFINE THE PURPOSE: Meditate on the life you are leaving behind and the new one you are embracing. Journal your thoughts if it helps. Talk it out with people close to you. Talk it out with your goddess or god ally. Rehearse the ritual in your mind.

DESIGN A GOOD RITUAL: Unless every step is traditional and immutable, you will need to get creative. Put something on paper, then ask yourself whether it feels powerful and right. Then ask whether it is a good ritual, let alone a good rite of passage. Is it appealing or dramatic visually, auditorily, and kinesthetically? Then make sure it has the following elements:

- INCLUDE A CHALLENGE: If the rite is mostly about changing your lifestyle, rather than immediate survival, don't make the ritual too easy on yourself. It needs to include some challenging, if symbolic act, otherwise you may not feel you have "earned" the right to be—whatever. This does not apply, obviously, to situations that have their own inherent physical challenge: serious illness or injury, or dying.
- CLARITY ABOUT YOUR NEW ROLE: You need a clear understanding of your new role: a set of expectations and code of conduct, written by you with input from

your healers, clergy, teachers, friends, or elders. A job description for the new you.

- **APPROPRIATE OPPORTUNITIES FOR EMOTIONAL EXPRESSION:** You (and others close to you) may be feeling very strong emotions. That's okay. Leaving behind what's familiar and comfortable is at least uncomfortable, if not terrifying. You may need some quiet time and private space, a shoulder to cry on, or someone to talk to who has been through the same transition. Your family and friends may need this, too.

- **ACKNOWLEDGE THE LOSS AND THE GAIN:** Your feelings of loss, fear, or grief must be honored. At the same time, the ritual should remind you of the good things that lie ahead: your renewed health and energy, the continued support of those who love you... and if you are dying, perhaps even the end of pain, and reunion with loved ones that the next life will bring.

- **INCLUDE GREAT MUSIC:** Find music that reflects loss, joy, wonder, triumph, remembrance, whatever the dominant emotions are likely to be. Possibly your favorite recorded music may work for parts of the ritual, but ideally you can include some live music from talented friends who are there feeling the experience. You can even invite participants to sing along, and create the music together.

PREPARE THE RITUAL: Confer with any helpers involved, organize the logistics, find the right costume, clean the space, gather altar items, decorate if you wish... there's plenty to do.

PREPARATION OF THE COMMUNITY: Family, friends, leaders, community members—all need to be told what is expected of them, where to go and when, what to say, and their individual roles in the ceremony and afterwards.

PREPARE YOURSELF: Just beforehand, take a ritual cleansing bath, then ground and center.

PERFORM THE RITUAL: But remember that you don't have to follow your outline rigidly; go with the flow and trust and follow your instincts.

HAVE GOOD FOOD: If it seems right, provide refreshments appropriate to the occasion, or invite people to bring food and beverages. Food helps people ground and find their centers after a powerful experience, and gives them something to do. Just go easy on liquor: you don't want people drinking too much and getting loud or maudlin, distracting everyone from the real center of attention—you and your transition.

ASK FOR CONTINUING SUPPORT: This ritual is important, but the transition continues and you will need support. Ask friends and family for what you need, including to check in with you regularly afterwards. You may need a hug, a friendly ear, information, financial counseling, an evening of babysitting, or just continued prayers and good wishes.

ACT IN ACCORD (see Chapter 5).

Conclusion

Please note: though we provide examples of what you can do in ritual, please use these only as a starting point. Any ritual that you design may be more powerful for you that one someone else has

Chapter 3

designed. If you want to learn more about designing your own rituals, please see our book: *RitualCraft: Creating Rites for Transformation and Celebration.* Most importantly, don't try to be all formal, stiff, and official; follow your feelings and the energy flow of the moment. The ritual is for you and your deity ally, and if it feels good, you're doing it right.

Chapter 4
More Spiritual Techniques

In the last chapter, we looked at a number of ways to support your healing through ritual. In most cases, healing ritual will involve the god or goddess you have chosen to work with on your healing journey.

Organizing and performing ritual is not something we can do at the drop of a hat, and many other ways to support your healing blend more easily into your daily life. Some of them are similar to the techniques you used to deepen your relationship with your divine ally, and some are different. In each case, though, the aim is to move beyond making friends and to channel your deity's power into creating a more healthful life. Here are some of your options.

Daily Practice

Try to establish the habit of performing a spiritual practice each and every day that will help you heal. Your daily practice can include meditation, chanting, divination, prayer, lighting candles, or any other of your usual spiritual activities—but if you are sick or injured, every single one can be adapted to focus on healing.

If you are used to meditating, then meditate upon images of yourself in good health, and using your newfound strength and wellness in service to your family and community. If you like to choose a tarot card each morning for guidance in the day ahead, ask yourself how the energy of that image can help you to achieve better health. If you light a candle and ask for blessings and protection for your family, include yourself in that request.

Can any parts of your medical or health regimen be included in a daily spiritual practice? For example, if you must take medications each day, why not thank your deity for your medication and then charge the medicines with a little magickal energy to boost the effect? If you have physical therapy exercises to do, instead of doing them mechanically while you watch television, envision yourself strong and whole and doing them more easily every day. Every time you do anything that the doctor or healer ordered, ask yourself, "How can I make this more vivid and powerful, and connect it with my spiritual path?"

Many of the techniques below can become a daily practice.

Breathing

Yoga practitioners practice pranayama, which includes several different kinds of intentional breathing exercises. If you think that breathing is a healthful thing, then make it even better by learning some of these exercises and practicing them whenever you have an idle moment. They are, variously, techniques for calming and relaxation, for focusing the mind, for energizing your body, and other purposes; but they all have the side benefit of bringing more oxygen into your body's cells.

Books on pranayama exist, but it may be easier for you to use recordings on the Internet or on CDs so you are not trying to read

More Spiritual Techniques

and learn the techniques at the same time. One example of a useful recording is Dr. Andrew Weil's *Breathing: The Master Key to Self-Healing*.

When you do the breathing, begin by asking the support of your divine partner in doing the exercises correctly and gaining maximum benefit; and end by thanking your deity for their help in this, and in all aspects of your healing.

Moving Energy

A healing approach that is common in many parts of the world, but well ignored in Western society, is to know your own energy field and do intentional maintenance work to keep it in good shape. Most people in the West have at least heard of things like chakras and auras, but few understand them very well or work with them regularly. Even if you cannot see or "read" energy fields, you do have one, and to ignore it is as silly as ignoring your stomach because you can't see it.

If this whole idea is new to you, then get some instruction and start learning how to sense your energy field. Plenty of books, CDs, and DVDs cover chakra work, although personal instruction from a yoga teacher or another practitioner is of course ideal. And if you still have trouble seeing your energy field or chakras after some training, don't worry: there are other ways to sense energy that are not visual. Some people hear different tones or vibrations for each chakra, other people can feel the differences, as textures, differences in temperature, or movement of air.

Once you are a little familiar with your energy field, then you can start learning ways to maintain and improve it. A popular

51

exercise mentioned in the last chapter is the Middle Pillar (see Appendix D), which feeds energy to each major chakra in turn and helps to clear, balance, and connect them. Reiki energy healing is another good way to work with your energy body as well as your physical body; there is a certain amount of mystique around the art of Reiki, and some schools charge quite a bit to train you in the techniques. However, remember that energy healing is part of our human heritage; anyone can learn to do it, and not all teachers charge large fees.

Each time you begin working with energy, in any form or using any technique, begin by asking your deity's help, and end with thanking them.

Color and Light

You may recall that we suggested wearing colors special to your deity in the chapter on building a relationship with your ally. Wearing those colors on a regular basis will remind you that you have an ally. If you know certain colors are flattering to your complexion and figure, wear those so that you feel more confident. If some colors just cheer you up and make you feel good, flattering or not, wear those as well!

You are probably aware that certain wavelengths of light are better for your health than others. Natural sunlight is obviously the best kind of light for you, provided you don't get sunburned. Call upon Apollo or Ra, Amaterasu or Helios, sun deities who can help with healing. Use lights in your home that feel comfortable and easy on your eyes. Electric bulbs that simulate the wavelength of natural sunlight are especially important if you are affected by

Seasonal Affective Disorder (SAD), which is fairly common in northern latitudes during the winter months when we don't get as much sunlight as our bodies and minds like. However; in your home, don't use any kind of lighting that feels harsh or unnatural.

Self-Talk

Most of us have a lot to tell ourselves, and some of it isn't pretty. We pick up on negative messages—often when we are very young—and repeat them to ourselves for years or even a lifetime. They can range from "I have no head for math" to "I'm such an idiot!" to "I'll never get well." When we believe such trash-talk about ourselves, these comments can become a self-fulfilling prophecy: you behave as if they are true, and your actions (or lack of them) make them come true.

And negative talk, whether from inside or outside, has an immediate physical effect. You may feel unloved or even threatened: your muscles tense, your blood diverts from your brain and internal organs, and even your biochemistry changes. You may think to yourself, as Charlie Brown does when he is slighted or criticized, "My stomach hurts." Over time these physiological reactions will cause your immune system to become compromised, and your health to deteriorate.

You cannot always change the thoughtless, malicious, and hurtful comments of others—although a bit of assertiveness with a goddess or god to back you up can work wonders. But you certainly can control your own messages to yourself. When you catch yourself muttering (or thinking) a put-down at yourself, instantly imagine that your patron god or goddess is present and listening. Then imagine what your divine ally—your wise, loving, compassionate ally—would say to you... perhaps, "You are too hard on yourself, my friend. Do not say such things to yourself; instead, think of all the good you have done, and will do, and heal yourself so that you may yet do more."

Affirmations and Afformations

This leads us to another form of self-talk: carefully crafted messages to yourself. Probably you are familiar with the growth tool called affirmations. These are statements like "My body takes me everywhere easily and effortlessly," or "I am in perfect health," two examples from Louise Hay's website.[2]

Many people have found this kind of affirmation to be very effective if repeated often enough, with conviction. However, others cannot say them with conviction: when they try, a little voice inside immediately reacts with something like "What? Who am I trying to kid? My hip hurts like hell when I try to walk, and that ain't perfect health."

An alternative technique is to create "afformations," the concept of author and speaker Noah St. John.[3] Instead of telling yourself something that's blatantly not true at the moment, ask yourself a question. Questions intrigue us, and we tend to try to answer them. So if you ask, "Why am I feeling a little stronger and healthier each day?" your mind will accept the stronger and healthier as fact, and look for the answers to the question posed:

---

[2] Louise Hay is the well-known author of *Heal Your Body*, that explores "the mental causes of physical ailments." See her website at http://www.louisehay.com/affirmations/#.

[3] For more about afformations, see Noah St. John's *Afformations®: The Miracle of Positive Self-Talk*. Hay House, 4th edition, 2014.

"Well, maybe because I'm doing those exercises the physical therapist gave me..." or "Because I'm getting lots of rest and time to heal...." or "I've got a great medical team AND my 'secret weapon,' a goddess who's determined I'm going to get better." If affirmations haven't worked for you, try afformations.

Conversation

This leads us to another form of communication: simply hold a conversation with your goddess or god. Looking at your end alone, it seems a lot like prayer—but we hope more thoughtful than the average prayer, which tends to include a certain amount of whining about the petitioner's troubles, followed by a request for divine intervention to fix them. Instead, at the very least, you might thank the deity for what's good in your life, and ask for help in understanding why you are being challenged in this way.

Then, the hard part: listening for the reply. Deity rarely speaks out loud in commanding tones: "Noah, I want you to build me an ark!" Messages from Spirit are more likely to come in the form of a quiet, gradual blossoming of understanding, or a gentle change in your feelings, or even an answer to the question you didn't ask, but should have. If you are very attuned to nature, the response may be revealed in the shift of the wind, or the flight of a bird, or the pattern of clouds: signs too subtle for most people to read. Patience and an open heart and mind will most likely bring understanding.

Chapter 4

Gratitude Journal

Finally, in the realm of words, consider starting a gratitude journal. The simple act of regularly (daily) expressing gratitude to deity for all the things that are going right in your life can soon create major changes in your life. When life seemed overwhelming a few years ago, Azrael began a gratitude journal. Her anxiety level went down within a week, and she began to feel better about her place in life and got clarity about where she wanted to go, and what she wanted to do. Other people have noticed ulcers diminishing, blood pressure lowering, and overall stress decreasing, uncomfortable relationships transforming, and the stresses of life becoming more manageable.

Begin with a blank journal, and first thing in the morning, or last thing at night, give gratitude for your blessings.

Azrael's recommendations for a gratitude journal include:

- Don't date the pages. It doesn't matter what date you are giving thanks, and if you do skip a day or two, you don't have the lack of the previous day's date berating you. Include only those things for which you are grateful, and the date in the upper corner is not one of them, necessarily.
- Write a whole page every day. It doesn't have to be a large journal—in fact, you may want to purposely begin with a small one, so a whole page is not so intimidating at first.
- Write in your own handwriting—this is not a place for computer entries. Studies have shown that there is a connection between writing by hand and physiological

and psychological changes in the brain that cannot be replicated by keyboarding.
- Begin with something like, "The Goddess provides." (Or Lady, or God, or the name of your ally.) This becomes a daily reminder that we don't have to provide everything for ourselves; we've got a major helper.
- Follow that with the words Thank you, Goddess. (or God, or Lady, or Lord, or the name of your ally). This gives credit where it is due.
- On the next line, write Thank you for _____, and fill in the blank. Azrael's first thanks is always for Amber.
- On the next line, write Thank you for _____, and fill in the blank. Continue until the whole page is filled.
- Your thanks can be for big things (Thank you for my surgery going so well.) Or for small things (Thank you for rocky road ice cream.) Mix in the big and small.
- At the bottom of the page, thank your deity once more, and close the book until the next day.

Journaling

That versatile tool, journaling, returns again. You used it as you built a relationship with your special god or goddess; now continue it to express your feelings about your situation, brainstorm new approaches to healing, record your experiences, and express your hopes.

Writing about your pain, your fears, and your anger can provide real catharsis—and it is healing to have negative emotions on a written page instead of eating you up inside. You can write down stuff that you would rather not share aloud, even with close family members. Nobody has to see it except you and your spirit ally. If you choose, you can tear out the negative pages, and burn them, destroying the power of those words and releasing them from your life.

However, challenge yourself to include optimistic ideas and dreams as well: Note signs of healing progress, comment on the people who are doing their best to help you, and note other strategies that might boost your health (a daily "green" drink as a healing "potion"?). Return to these positive pages, and re-read what you wrote. Note the gradual (or sudden) increases in wellness and capability that have occurred as you've worked with your deity over the course of days, weeks, or months. Noting the changes will increase the pace at which change occurs.

If you believe you are dying, would you rather focus on all that you are losing… or on the possibility of a wondrous afterlife, where you will reunite with old friends, beloved family members, and cherished animal companions? Describe it in the most glowing terms you can imagine, and imagine your ally there to greet and guide you!

Amulets and Talismans

Design an amulet or talisman to represent the healing power of your goddess or god. What's the difference? An amulet can be described as "a small object worn to ward off evil, harm, or illness or to bring good fortune; a protecting charm," whereas a talisman is more specifically "a stone, ring, or other object, engraved with figures or characters supposed to possess occult powers and worn as an amulet or charm."[4]

Thus, the term "amulet" is more general, and for many magickal practitioners usually means a natural object such as an acorn (representing a god like Zeus, Odin, or the Oak King) or a stone with a natural hole in it (symbolizing a mother goddess such as Ishtar, Inanna, or Bona Dea). Talismans, on the other hand, often take the form of jewelry with magickal or sacred symbols on them: perhaps the name of your divine ally in their "native language," whether it be cuneiform, Greek, or the Norse runes.

Whatever you choose or create, you can either wear it 24/7, or just during your daily spiritual practice at your shrine or altar. (Much depends on the duration and nature of your illness.) As an example, Azrael wore either a tourmaline crystal (to filter out unintentional fear- or worry-vibes when people sent her healing energy; a rose quartz pendant for general blessing energy and quick convalescence, or a midnight pyrite pendant (dark blue with sparkles)[5] to represent Nuit, the Egyptian goddess of the night sky who was Azrael's healing ally for the duration of her breast cancer hobby.

An amulet or talisman is always more effective when it is charged with energy, as discussed in Chapter 3 on ritual. Whether you charge it with the energy of your ally, the Earth, the Moon, the Sun, the stars, or simply the ambient energy field, do remember to refresh the charge at least once each week—daily is better.

---

[4] www.dictionary.com. p.s., Occult simply means "hidden."
[5] She could have used lapis lazuli or blue goldstone; many options are available when you are working with magickal jewelry.

Chapter 4

Making Offerings

Common gifts to deity include food, beverages, and incense; and used to include blood sacrifices—which we do NOT recommend.

If you cannot find foods or incenses specific to your god or goddess, then choose ones from the culture and era in which their worship arose. Outdoors, you may simply leave the food on the altar, where a hungry squirrel can enjoy it later on behalf of the deity. A liquid offering can simply be poured on to the earth, with appropriate words of gratitude. In the case of incense, the smoke can carry your desires aloft to the spirit realms.

Giving service to your deity in gratitude for their help is one of the best kinds of offerings. Give your energy, talents, and resources to a cause that aligns with your god's or goddess' nature: give a good herbal healing book to someone in Airmed's name, or throw a bright and festive party in Beiwe's name in the cold darkness of winter, or clean out a wild hot spring for Grannus.

If your medical condition rules out any physically active service, maybe you could make a donation to the American Heart Association in Cardea's name, or simply write a letter of appreciation to any healer or health organization: a little gratitude helps keep them going.

Chanting

Creating music, even a simple chant or plainsong, engages both sides of the brain, makes us breathe more deeply, and creates a thing of beauty. It's a great way to express thanks and share our deepest emotions... and you know your special goddess or god is listening, and loving it.

Once, long ago, all musical expression was ephemeral, because there was no way to record music at all. When the shaman set aside her drum, or the bard put down his harp, the music they made lasted only in memory. Later, music could be preserved in the dry form of musical notation, but no performance or interpretation was captured. Now we have high-quality recordings, and can listen to the uplifting and healing music all day long, go to sleep to it, and even preserve our own musical endeavors for our descendants. Whether you listen to music or create it, or both, factor it into your healing program.

Visualization, Meditation, Guided Meditation

We have discussed meditation as one way to forge a relationship with your divine ally; but don't stop there. Continue to visualize yourself getting stronger and healthier day by day... doing tasks you could not handle last week... feeling pain fade away and a sense of well-being growing.

Your guided meditations (whether written and recorded by yourself, or led by a friend) can take you to places in your mind where the gods touch you with healing power, and fresh air and natural beauty cleanse your spirit, and brilliant lights and colors flow through your energy body and reinvigorate your self-healing abilities. Use your mind and imagination to smooth the way to wellness!

Chapter 4

Dance

The rhythmic use of your whole body is a healthful thing, and dance moves beyond simple calisthenics to a pattern of beauty that expresses joy, gratitude, communion, freedom, seduction, or any number of happy things. Depending on the shape you're in, your movements may be halting and awkward at first, but never mind—strength and grace will come with practice—and the only ones watching are your allies, and they love you for your dance.

If dancing with your whole body is not an option, then dance with your fingers, or even simply in your mind. Enough for now: at a future time—or lifetime—you will do more.

Dreamwork

Before you retire for the night, drink a soothing cup of herbal tea (mugwort tea enhances dreams), and meditate on the dreams you'll have. Will you visit your spirit ally in some special place (shrine, tavern, or forest grove) and talk about your life and plans? Will you visit a healing temple of ancient times and let the wise priests and priestesses work their magick upon you? Will you send your mind and spirit into your own body and explore the issues for yourself, from the inside?

Remember, the moment you wake, take just a few minutes to record all you can remember about your dreams (have a notebook, journal, or recording device ready). Thinking upon them later may give you new insights into your healing journey.

Labyrinth

Walk a labyrinth with your deity. If you are not familiar with labyrinths, read a book about them and see if you are attracted to the idea. Humans have built and walked labyrinths for thousands of years, all over the world... and yet their purpose and effects are still a mystery. At the very least, they seem to relieve stress and quiet the mind so that new insights and understandings can rise to consciousness. But they may also be a way to mentally "unmake" and "recreate" the self, a form of spiritual releasing and renewal. When you do walk the labyrinth, release what you do not need on the way in. Your ally can meet you in the center, and will have a message for you, so pause, and really listen. Then, on the way out, accept what you need to go forward.

Again, if you cannot physically walk a labyrinth outdoors, you can trace one on paper (or carved into wood) with your finger, or just your eyes. However you manage it, take your divine ally along and let them guide you and even offer commentary.

Retreat

If you're not confined to a hospital or your home, consider "getting away from it all" to someplace quiet and private where you can simply breathe deeply and focus on your healing. Borrow an unused cabin or guesthouse from a friend, or head to a resort or a little bed-and-breakfast if you can afford it. Leave the petty distractions and chores of your usual life behind, and let responsibility slip from your shoulders. Take a trusted and loved

Chapter 4

companion with you, if you could use a helper or just good company. And, of course, meet your ally there, too.

And we'll say it again: if you can't take your body to a wonderful retreat place, you can still go there in your mind. Watch or listen to a fun travel video about someplace you've always wanted to visit. The British Isles? A tropical island? The Swiss Alps? Then go there in your head, creating as much detail—color, sounds, textures, smells, tastes, and feelings—as you can. These inner excursions have great advantages: they are extremely inexpensive, and absolutely tailored to what *you* need.

Pilgrimage

For a retreat, you want anyplace that's quiet and relaxing, in pleasant or hopefully beautiful surroundings. For a pilgrimage, you'll want a destination that's spiritually meaningful and powerful. A Christian might choose Lourdes, where the Virgin Mary appeared; or a great cathedral; or of course the Holy Land. Ask yourself, "What place is special to my goddess or god ally?"

If you are working with Brigit, many holy wells are dedicated to her, especially in Ireland; and, in particular, at the site of her abbey at Kildare. Visit a temple to Apollo in Delphi, Greece, or one of the many other sites where he was worshipped. If your ally is Mati Syra Zemlya, head for the valley of the Don River (in Russia, northeast of the Black Sea) where she was first known. If Nodens is your god, you can see the remains of his temple complex at Lydney Park in England. Find a temple to Sitala in India, or for Tawaret travel to the temple of Ipet at Karnak in Egypt. or to Kerma, the ancient capital of Nubia.

If you don't have the money or mobility to visit these holy places, you can find videos of sacred places and take a "virtual pilgrimage." Be sure to include meditation, offerings, ritual, or anything else you would include in a physical pilgrimage.

Conclusion

Every time you take any action to heal yourself, ask yourself these questions: When I do receive the gifts of wellness, strength, and energy; what will I use them for? Why do I even want vibrant health if I have no plans, dreams, or visions to strive toward? If I want the gift of more hours or years here on earth, how will I use them? What *are* my plans, visions, and dreams? To desire more life only because you fear death seems very sad to us. The gift of life is a great one, and should be used for great purposes. Find your purpose, and your deity ally will help you achieve it.

Chapter 5
Acting in Accord

Magick is wonderful, enriching, empowering, powerful, and life-changing. But doing magick is only half or less of the work the magician does. The other half, after the magick spell, is the work on the mundane plane, called *acting in accord*. It is just as important as the magick, and is indispensable to the result.

Some books intimate that all you have to do is visualize what you want and believe with all your being that you have it, and it will manifest in your life. That is like a small child believing that "If I just wish hard enough, I'll get a pony!"

True magick just isn't that simple. From a religious perspective, we could say "The gods help those that help themselves"—and if they don't see you doing something to support the magick, they will not help manifest the desired result. They will assume that you are unwilling to put in some sweat equity to assist the process.

Acting in accord includes all the steps you take on the physical plane, to manifest your desire in this reality.

So, for healing, what does acting in accord look like once you've connected with the healing deity, developed a relationship, and done rituals or spells to align yourself with their power?

Chapter 5

Inhabiting a Body: Really Basic Stuff

Eat right, exercise regularly, get enough sleep yada yada yada. You've heard these before—they're not new. But **this basic health self-care list is now your absolute top priority in life.**

Yes, you have other responsibilities: taking care of people you love, your job, etc. But you can't fulfill ANY of those responsibilities if you're really sick, injured, or dead. Airplane analogy: put your oxygen mask on first, then help the kids.

So, if you plan to heal, this list is now Numbers 1-12 on your life's "To Do" list. We have named the list after Nike, the Greek goddess of success. As she says, "Just do it."[6]

Nike's Twelve

1. BREATHE CLEAN AIR. Stop smoking, if you still do. If you live in a smoggy city, get out (move) or use air filters in your home and a mask outside. If your workplace has toxic air, make a ruckus until management cleans it up.
2. DRINK ENOUGH CLEAN WATER. Yes, most tap water is okay, but some is very much not okay. Use a home water filter, or better still, get your town to adopt tough water quality standards for tap water. Stay hydrated.
3. EAT NOURISHING FOOD. Whatever that is, right? Well, start with local, preferably organic vegetables, then add grass-fed meat, poultry and seafood, fruit in moderation,

---

[6] This book does not provide medical advice. Consult a healthcare professional prior to beginning any exercise or diet program, or any treatment for a health issue.

and the good oils: nuts, avocado, coconut, and olive. Reduce sugar, salt, and artificial ingredients WAY down, and you're pretty much there.

4. GET ENOUGH SLEEP. The amount varies according to your age and condition. Six to eight hours nightly? Ask your body: How much sleep leaves you feeling your best? And in what pattern? Some people thrive on "power naps," or on breaking their nightly rest into two chunks.

5. LIVE IN A HEALTHY HOME. It could be an apartment, a ranch house, a stone tower, or a Mongolian-style yurt. But well-heated if it's cold outside, well-ventilated if it's not, free of household chemicals, fire hazards, vermin, and noisy neighbors. Clean, neat, and attractive are bonuses.

6. EXERCISE REGULARLY. Many experts now say that we need three kinds of exercise for optimum health: cardio (increases heart rate), strength (builds muscle), and flexibility (stretches joints and ligaments). If you can't run five miles, hit the barbells, and do hatha yoga daily—okay, sick or injured—then do what you can; even tiny amounts of exercise, done frequently, add up fast.

7. WEAR THE RIGHT CLOTHING. Meaning mostly natural fibers, enough to protect yourself from hot sun or cold conditions. And wear comfy shoes. Yes, fashion is important—well, not very, especially if you're sick—but get your priorities straight.

8. TAKE SAFETY PRECAUTIONS. Put solid locks on your home. Maintain your car properly. Avoid dangerous stuff like getting drunk, doing illegal drugs, or swimming in shark-infested waters.

These are the most immediate, physical needs that you need in order to heal. If you are too sick to do these things, you need to get help NOW: call in all your "markers," with family, friends, associates, support people private and professional—and get their help. This is no time to be cussedly independent. Besides, people like to feel needed and valued; they would LIKE to help you (unless you're such a total schmuck that everyone wants you dead; how likely is that?). And their helping you is a step in their own self-transcendence (see number 12).

The following needs are important, but are difficult to focus on if you need physical healing. However, keeping them in mind and working towards them will contribute to your healing—you'll heal better and faster if you can satisfy them, or even make a little progress on each one.

9. LOVE, AND BELONG. Find someone or something to love; if you're not partnered and don't have kids, love a dog or a bird. Belong to something: a 4-H center, a geology club, a "friends of the library" association, a Scout troop. Isolation hurts your health. (But if you're contagious, please don't socialize until the contagion is gone.)

10. LIKE AND RESPECT YOURSELF. This is permitted even if you haven't achieved perfection. In fact, it's allowed even if you've mostly been a screw-up all your life so far. Start by treating other people well, and doing something you can be proud of. And don't diss yourself out of habit; skip that negative self-talk, and do better tomorrow.

11. IMPROVE YOURSELF. According to Abraham Maslow, once the basics of physical health, safety, love and belonging, and self-esteem have been achieved, then you

can work on *self-actualization*. That means developing your talents and skills, so that you are a better, stronger, more skilled and resourceful person over time, in service to yourself and others. In short, fulfilling your own potential. Maybe that's not uppermost in your mind if you're very ill, but at least keep it on the back burner for when you get better—something to look forward to!

12. SELF-TRANSCENDENCE. Maslow's original hierarchy of needs had self-actualization as the apex toward which we all strive, once our other needs are met. In later life, Maslow developed an additional level, which he called *self-transcendence*. Living just for yourself is insufficient; true actualization is only possible when you are giving to some higher goal outside yourself. It means giving and relating to yourself, yes, but also to your "significant others, to human beings in general, to other species, to nature, and to the entire cosmos." It brings in the concepts of altruism and spirituality that were mostly not present in his original hierarchy.[7]

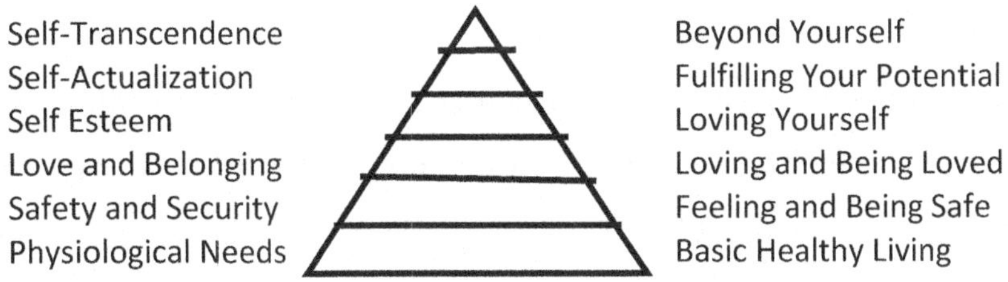

Self-Transcendence		Beyond Yourself
Self-Actualization		Fulfilling Your Potential
Self Esteem		Loving Yourself
Love and Belonging		Loving and Being Loved
Safety and Security		Feeling and Being Safe
Physiological Needs		Basic Healthy Living

Maslow's Revised Hierarchy

---

[7] Maslow, Abraham. *The Farther Reaches of Human Nature*. Viking, New York, 1971, p. 269.

Chapter 5

Another Take on Human Needs

Author Susan Fowler[8] explains three basic needs that overlap with Maslow's hierarchy. The first is *autonomy*. An autonomous person perceives that they have choices, that they act of their own volition, and that their actions are their own, not at someone else's command. This means you feel free to make decisions about your life.

In the normal course of events, this would include decisions on where to live or travel, what kind of work to do, whether to get more education, how to manage your time, and so on. (It's relative: people who live in community are never perfectly free, because they have to respect others' freedoms.)

When you're ill or injured, autonomy also means that you have some choice about which doctor you'll see, what kind of treatment you'll receive, whether you'll recover at home or in a medical facility, what kind of meals you'll be given, and so on. Medical and health care professionals may offer you choices, but if they don't—if you're treated like meat, in the worst case—then you may need an advocate to speak up for you and demand that you be given respect, information, and choices.

Fowler also discusses *relatedness*: a need to be connected to others, to care about and be cared about, without concerns about ulterior motives, and to feel that one is contributing to something greater than oneself.

This connects to Maslow's idea that we all need love and belonging, to love and be loved. Especially when we are vulnerable

---

[8] Fowler, Susan. *Why Motivating People Doesn't Work... and What Does.* Berrett-Koehler Publishers, 2017.

and fragile, we want people around us who really care about us on a personal level, as well as those who care in a competent, professional way. Ask for the presence of friends and family, and folks from your religious community, even people from work that you are close to. You might be surprised how many people care enough to come around when you need some support.

The second part of relatedness, contributing to something greater, relates to Maslow's self-transcendence, and may be really hard when we're feeling low. There will be times, and maybe long stretches of time, when you must lie back and let others take care of you, and trust them also to cope with the big world's issues. Perhaps your contribution, your service, consists of a smile, a whispered "Thank you" to a nurse, or a quiet "Hang in there" to your hospital roommate. You can only do what you can; just remember, any kind of giving helps you as well as the recipient.

Fowler's third area of human need is *competence*, a "need to feel effective at meeting every-day challenges and opportunities, demonstrating skill over time, and feeling a sense of growth and flourishing."

This is a tough one to work on when you're hurt or sick. Physically you may not be able to handle the usual daily challenges or demonstrate your normal skills, and you're certainly not flourishing. So, how do you handle your feelings of frustration and helplessness?

A couple of things might help. First, remember that you have proven your skills and competence throughout your life. What you accomplished counts toward who you are and will be again. Unless your condition is terminal, unless you are dying, you need to believe that you can be a competent, self-reliant person again.

And if you are dying? You still leave a legacy of all that you accomplished when you were well. That was and is real. It made a difference to your family, friends, and community. Reflect on what you did, what you can be proud of.

If your spiritual beliefs include reincarnation, then be sure that you will once again be young, strong, confident, skilled, and competent. Your story isn't over, even if a chapter ends.

Competence also includes *growth*. Can you grow as a person while you're ill? Yes. You can grow in compassion, understanding, courage, and spirit. You may not be earning a Master's degree or learning karate, but the most important growth happens in our hearts, and doesn't require physical strength or agility.

Add Yourself to Your Healing Team

You will doubtless involve medical and health professionals if you are very ill or injured. Your healing team may include "conventional" or allopathic medical folks: your family physician, a nurse practitioner, a surgeon, a physical therapist, and others—and perhaps "alternative" healing professionals providing acupuncture, chiropractic, and more.

Make sure both sets of healers—conventional and alternative—know what you're doing on your own and with the others. You do NOT need multiple clashing treatments that confuse or actually harm your body's natural healing processes. And some treatments that are fine alone may do real damage in combination with others. In other cases, a treatment from one tradition or field will support and augment something else. A team can only work as a team if each player knows what the others are doing.

But wait—we said "what you're doing on your own and with the others." You must do Nike's Twelve—basic maintenance—but you can do more than that. You can learn a healing modality and become a healer yourself; then use your new skills first on yourself, and later share them with others.

We are not suggesting that you run out (or maybe crawl out, considering) and enroll in medical school, aiming to become a brain surgeon in your spare time. We are suggesting that while you're resting and recuperating, in between treatments, you begin to explore some healing modality that interests you. There is an ancient archetype called the "Wounded Healer," referring to one who is grievously injured or disabled yet reaches out to help heal others. Maybe that's you. Maybe you have some healing talent, and combined with your experiences right now as a "patient," you can help others down the road... and even before that, yourself.

All humans have actual and potential healing ability, beginning with our inborn body wisdom that causes our cells to fight off infection, bruises to fade, and bleeding to clot. Without the body's impulse to heal, our species would have been extinct long ago.

We also have the potential to learn skills and techniques that support the body's instinctive urge toward health. Some people take years of training and become medical professionals, others learn just enough first aid to take care of their children's everyday "owies." Some study herb-craft and can make healthful teas and tinctures from local plants; others get training in yogic energy exercises that strengthen their chakras.

Some are educated as psychotherapists or family counselors, while others develop a knack for listening and gentle questioning that makes them effective peer counselors. Some are self-taught nutritional experts, while others go to massage school and become the saviors of sore and tight muscles.

You don't have to attend an expensive college or commit to a new profession in order to understand the human body better—and its relationship with the mind, emotions, energy field, social network, environment, etc. This is information that everyone on the planet should have, and few are lucky enough to learn thoroughly in school.

Beyond that, maybe you have a real aptitude for Reiki energy healing, or herbal medicine, or color therapy, or any one of a hundred other healing modalities. See the list in Appendix C, and consider whether one sounds intriguing. Read a basic book on that, catch an introductory YouTube video, and see where your needs and passions take you.

The Golden Pentacle

A good framework for manifestation is the Golden Pentacle, which Azrael developed and which we are writing a whole book about, focused mainly on prosperity. However, the process can be used to achieve any goal, including healing.

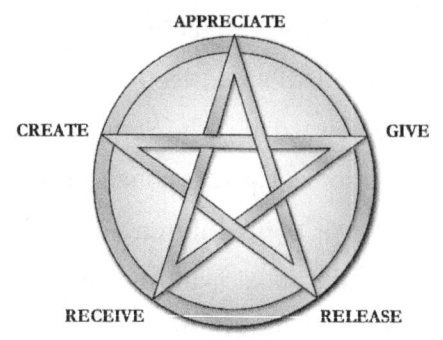

At the top is the first and most important point, APPRECIATE. Daily appreciation of what you have will lay a firm foundation for change. When the gods know that you appreciate what you already have, they are more likely to grant your desires for more. So, if you have the flu, and are working magick for healing and wellness, first be grateful that you are alive, have clean water to drink, clean air to breathe through your stuffed-up nose, that your dog is staying right beside you, that the flowers outside your window are bright and cheerful, that you have enough sick leave to see you through this, etc. Be sure to write at least a page of appreciation every day—listing things and people you are grateful for, thanking the gods and goddesses for what you have.

Doing this in writing is important because it keeps you focused on what you are doing, and keeps your mind from wandering. Writing manually, pen or pencil on paper, rather than inputting to a computer, also makes a direct channel to the brain, engaging both body and mind.

The second point of the Golden Pentacle is to RELEASE. This can mean releasing physical things, mental ideas, emotional attachments or negative emotions, bad habits, negative or unsupportive people, or even an unhealthy home or job. What is your ailment? If it is an illness, what physical things could you release to help bring relief? For instance, getting back to the flu, if you release alcohol for the duration, your immune system won't be distracted by that foreign substance, and can focus on healing you faster. Ask your deity or Divine Array what you need to release, and then do it.

With a chronic condition, like chemical sensitivities, you may even need to release your home and find a healthy place to live.

If your job is hazardous, and has led to a predictable injury or illness, you may have to release that job and find a new one.

What about releasing emotional ties or habits? Lung cancer is pretty obvious—give up, release, the cigarettes and the emotional

Chapter 5

need for them. Not easy, but possible. And release doesn't have to be done alone—get help from your healthcare practitioner, a counselor, and a friend. Ask your deity for help—do magick and ritual, and ditch the cigarettes in ritual.

The third step, after release, is to CREATE. Again, this can be physical, mental, emotional, or spiritual. You may need to create a different physical reality—create, or have a contractor create, ramps in your home if you have mobility issues, create an exercise program to strengthen your weak back (call on Osiris for help), create a new way of eating if you have diabetes, and so forth.

Create a group of supporters if you are dealing with a mental or emotional issue. A therapist (or psychiatrist if drugs are part of the therapy), your primary health care provider, your friends and family, and your deity or Divine Array together comprise your support team. At the same time, create a less stressful life if you can, because stress aggravates most mental conditions. Cut out unnecessary commitments; create space and time to breathe.

The next step is to GIVE. Once again, giving can be physical, monetary, mental, emotional, spiritual, or your time.

Money is easy: give to causes that support research into what ails you. You may already be receiving the benefits of other people's giving, so pay it back. You may not get a cure for Parkinson's, but someone else may benefit in five years, because you donated today.

Give your knowledge to someone else, your emotional stability to someone in crisis, your deep faith in the gods to someone in spiritual distress, your time and energy to whoever needs it. When you give, give—at least internally—in the name of your chosen deity. Even if you're quite ill, you may still be able to give of yourself, even if it's listening to a friend's problem rather than dumping your own anguish on them.

The fifth step is to RECEIVE, because once you've appreciated, released, created, and given, you *will* receive. The Threefold Law kicks in: what you send out, you receive back threefold. So all that energy you spent will return to you, magnified. Sending out energy in physical ways—like releasing your old, toxic house and creating a new nontoxic house—will reap positive physical results.

If you were working on the emotional plane, your emotional health will improve threefold. The same with the spiritual plane, and especially with money matters—but that's a different book. Now you move back to APPRECIATION; expand and repeat.

Let's go through two examples of working the Golden Pentacle in healing: one illness and one injury.

For the illness, let's choose diabetes as an example. Diabetes is high blood sugar to the point of being unhealthy, and even dangerous if untreated. First, create a relationship with a god or goddess of healing. In this case you will probably choose a general healing deity, since diabetes was uncommon before the 18th century, and most of the gods and goddesses predate that. So, let's choose Hygeia, Greek goddess of health, cleanliness, and sanitation; she is appropriate because you going to have to clean up your diet to get to health. After you've read her myths, created an altar and a talisman to charge and carry with you, and done some magick, then what?

First, APPRECIATE. This you know how to do—it's simple, but mandatory. Appreciate what you have in writing daily; write at least one full page. Appreciate that Hygeia is willing to work with you and walk with you to a better life, with diabetes under control.

Chapter 5

Second, RELEASE. This may be the hardest part for diabetics. Release all the white flour and refined sugar, all the simple carbohydrates. Ask Hygeia if anything else in your cupboards or refrigerator is making you sick, and act on what she says.

Also release your emotional dependence on cupcakes, pies, and candy as a way of feeling loved. Release your habit of accepting those from others as their way of expressing love. Release also your dislike of exercise (you'll be doing a lot more of it from now on). Release anything else that stands in the way of perfect health, including any fear of going to the doctor.

Now CREATE, with Hygeia, a new menu of exciting, healthy options for your meals; get help from the many websites and books on the subject. Create a whole repertoire of delicious, healthy things to eat. You will find new recipes to use with your cupcake tins and pie tins, too!

Create an exercise program that you will enjoy. Perhaps your spirituality is deeply rooted in the Earth. Go for long walks in nature, enjoying the miracle of that physical manifestation of the great Goddess—every day.

Create new ways to interact with friends (that don't include stopping at the doughnut shop). Perhaps a walk together, or window-shopping, or movie with a small popcorn only.

GIVE your time to a charity, and some money to the American Diabetes Association. If you can't stand seeing that Bundt pan in your cupboard, give it away. Ask Hygeia what else you can give.

RECEIVE good health, lower blood sugar numbers, and a sense of true accomplishment. With discipline and care, you may even receive the gift of getting off insulin, and staying off. Receive the gift of two-sizes-smaller clothes, and the admiration of friends and family. Receive Hygeia's love and approval. Receive a longer life, lived more fully.

APPRECIATE all that you have achieved, and let Hygeia know that you appreciate the help she gave you all along the way.

Repeat the Golden Pentacle as many times as necessary to achieve good health. In fact, make it your way of life by consciously working each point every day.

Next, we will choose the example of a strained back as the injury du jour, because back pain is among the most common problems in modern society. Let's choose Osiris, a god with a strong back to help out. You've developed a relationship, done ritual, and are now ready to act in accord.

APPRECIATE what you have in writing daily, at least one full page (you can use a small notebook at first, and work up to larger ones as you like). Appreciate that Osiris is willing to work with you and walk with you to a better life, with a healthy, happy back. Appreciate the times when your back does not hurt, and when it supports you physically to do things you want to do.

RELEASE bad habits that lead to back pain. Slouching at your computer in a chair with no back support? Release it! Lifting heavy objects using poor posture and poor lifting techniques? Stop that!

If you agree with author Louise Hay that every physical problem is tied to an emotional or mental cause, release any belief that you are not getting enough support in your life.

With Osiris, CREATE or learn a gentle exercise program such as Z-Health, that strengthens, loosens, and repairs joints and increases mobility. Create a less-stressful life, by decreasing the number of obligations you have.

Create a talisman for back health. An ancient Egyptian symbol called the "Tet of Osiris" represents the strength and stability of the spine, perfect for your purpose.

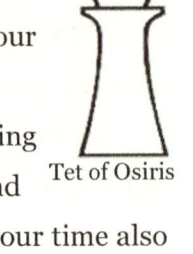

GIVE your time to yourself, for a change, by giving yourself opportunities to walk, get gentle exercise, and even do yoga or other joint-mobility exercises. Give your time also to others who are in worse health than you, and to organizations that promote good health.

Tet of Osiris

RECEIVE a stronger, healthier back. (Don't overdo the lifting, though!) Receive nights of peaceful sleep, and the ability to walk through your days pain-free.

Then APPRECIATE your "new" back, and Osiris for walking by your side to health. Repeat the Golden Pentacle as many times as it takes to get to your desired health.

Conclusion

The first step toward healing, is to enlist the aid of your divine partner, then incorporate Nike's 12 into your life—take care of yourself physically first, and work up Maslow's Hierarchy as you are able.

By working Nike's 12 and following the Golden Pentacle—appreciate, release, create, give, receive, appreciate, repeating the cycle—you are acting in accord with your magick, to heal whatever ails you. With your goddess, god, or Divine Array by your side, you can walk with assurance into a new, healthy life.

Now, what divine beings can help you? Join us as we explore a few dozen gods and goddesses whose specialty is healing.

SECTION TWO
The Goddesses and Gods of Healing

Part 1
Featured Gods and Goddesses

Thousands of deities from cultures around the world might be helpful to you, but to narrow the field we have chosen a few dozen, from many eras and civilizations, whose specialty is healing, or, in a few cases, powerful goddesses and gods who are best known for other qualities, but still include healing among their many talents. We have included their descriptions and their symbols, so that you may find inspiration for your healing altar or rituals.

Chances are one or more will have a special appeal for you. If not, we have a backup list of dozens more in Part 2.

Appendix A lists the gods and goddesses by healing specialty, or specific illness or injury. If you prefer to work with a deity from your own heritage or ancestral culture, check out Appendix B.

Names of other featured deities are in ALL CAPS.

Airmed: herbs, battle wounds, resurrection

Airmeath, Airmid

Europe, Celtic: Ireland

Airmed is the Irish goddess of herbal healing and a member of the Tuatha Dé Danann, who was renowned for her skill in healing those injured in battle. She could even revive the slain by singing powerful incantations over the well of Sláine, or Well of Health, which she helped create.

Her father, DIAN CÉCHT, killed her brother Miach out of envy of his surgical skills. Airmed wept over her brother's grave, and from her tears sprouted all the healing herbs of the world—365 of them, one for every organ and joint of the human body. Used correctly, they could even confer immortality on a patient.

The herbs spoke to Airmed, each explaining its special curative power and how it should be used. Airmed collected and arranged them all on her cloak, but then her father heard of her almost-miraculous healing powers, and in a jealous rage flung her cloak into the air, scattering the herbs over the earth. No human now knows the secrets of all the herbs, their locations or all their healing properties. Airmed alone remembers.

According to legend, Airmed fled deep into the mountains, and still lives in a solitary cottage there. She is visited by elves and faery folk who need healing, and the rare human determined enough to seek out her hidden dwelling.

Invoke the aid of Airmed if you plan to enlist the powers and spirits of medicinal herbs in your healing, if you have suffered a major injury, or if your condition is very serious. In meditation or dreams, seek Airmed in her remote cottage and ask her help.

Anahita: sacred sexuality, childbirth, sacred water

Anaheed, Anahit, Anaïtis, Ardwisur Anahid, Aredvi Sura Anahita, Nahid, and more

Asia and the Middle East, Persian

Anahita is an Indo-Iranian goddess of water, healing, wisdom, love, sacred sexuality, fertility, childbirth, and the moon. She is called The Golden Mother, and Anaïtis of the Sacred Water, and is a war goddess, driving a chariot with four white horses called Cloud, Hail, Rain, and Wind. Silver sculptures depict her as nude or wearing little, carrying flowers, fruit, children, and birds. Her symbols may have been a crenelated crown, and the sacred bull.

Her name means "pure" or "immaculate," and she is both the divine spirit of the mythical world river and also the source of all waters. She flows from the world mountain at the center of all things, the High Hara, where the sky turns on its pivot. The warm, pure water flows through a hundred thousand golden channels and nurtures all things, bringing life, health, and prosperity to the world. In time, it flows to the World Ocean, which bears up the Earth, and from there to all the lakes and seas.

She is also the planet Venus, which has been identified with life-giving goddesses since time immemorial.

One of her sanctuaries is described as a glorious temple of golden columns and silver tiles, shining and magnificent.

Anahita will help with fertility, and will bring the healing powers of water to your recovery from illness or injury, perhaps *watsu* water therapy, drinking pure water that is ritually charged, flower remedies, or even swimming to rebuild strength and flexibility. Seek her wherever the waters flow.

Section II, Part 1

Angitia: herbs, magick, snakebite

Anagtia, Anceta, Anguitia, Arigitia, Diiva

Mediterranean, Roman: Central Italy

Angitia is a goddess of healing, herbs, magick, and witchcraft (often all considered related), and is sister of the witch/sorceresses Circe and Medea; sometimes they are conflated.

She is also a snake goddess—in fact, the Romans derived her name from the word anguis, meaning "serpent." Snake-charmers claimed to descend from her bloodline. She has great powers over the reptiles, especially in healing snakebites. Snakes, of course, have been a symbol of regeneration and healing for millennia, and are linked with many goddesses of healing.

Ancient inscriptions tell of her temples, treasuries, and at least one sacred grove (the Forest of Angitia near the Fucine Lake in central Italy, now dry) where supplicants came to seek healing.

Enlist Angitia's help when you plan to use the ancient combination of herbcraft and ritual or spells to support the healing process. She excels in healing snakebites, but she can support you in any health issue, and will appreciate it if you create a shrine in her honor, perhaps beneath a special tree.

Apollo: sun, healing, plagues, wounds

Apollon, Apulu, Phoebus, and more
Mediterranean, Greek, Roman

Originally one of the Greek Olympians, Apollo is a god of healing, music, poetry, truth and prophecy, the sun and light, reason, inspiration, harmony, justice, archery, and plague (both bringing plague and healing it). He is the leader of the nine Muses, goddesses of music and the arts, as well as patron of colonists, flocks, and herds.

Apollo is depicted as a handsome, athletic youth, sometimes with a lyre (harp-like musical instrument), or occasionally driving the sun across the sky in his golden chariot. Apollo's symbols are the laurel tree, laurel wreath, swan, raven, and bow and arrow.

He is the son of Zeus and Leto; brother of the virgin huntress ARTEMIS; and lover to many of both sexes. He is father of many deities, including the great healer ASCLEPIUS.

As Pythian Apollo, he is the patron of the famous Oracle at Delphi, once dedicated to Gaia, where the priestesses, or oracles, entered a trance and offered cryptic messages from the god.

Among his dozens of titles, some are related to healing: Healer of Wounds, Protector from Plague, Helper, Apollo Acesius or Akestor (Averter of Evil), Apollo Medicus (Physician), Apollo Culicarius (He Who Drives Away Mosquitos/Midges), Apollo Vindonnus (Clear Light) who heals eyes, and many others.

His name Apollo Paean means Apollo Who Touches, but paean also meant a sacred song of protection and healing, or giving thanks for heaaling; a song sung by armies before battle and in thanks for victory; as well as the god who personified such songs.

Apollo was honored by every Greek and Roman. The Greeks sometimes conflated him with the Titan sun god Helios. In the western regions of the Empire, he was often equated with similar Celtic sun and horse gods.

Call Apollo if you or yours are injured, or if you want to harness the healing powers of sunlight and music, or if epidemics are abroad. In ritual, raise power by addressing him by his titles as healer: "Come now, O Lord of the Sun and Great Physician, you who are called Apollo Acesius, Apollo Akestor, Apollo Medicus, Apollo Paean, come to this circle where thy skills are needed!"

Artemis/Diana: fertility, childbirth, mental health, protector of women and children

Mediterranean, Greek, Roman

Though they are not exactly the same, Artemis (Greek) and Diana (Roman) share most of the same attributes, especially those related to healing. Artemis/Diana is the goddess of the hunt, wild animals, forests and mountains, the wilderness, secret sanctuaries in nature, fertility, childbirth, health and healing, mental health, woodland medicines, sports and exercise, and keen senses; she is the defender of girls and women. She may have originated long before classical Greek civilization, and is said to be the warrior goddess revered by the Amazons. Later in her career she became linked with the moon, as her twin brother, APOLLO, was with the sun.

Artemis' father is Zeus, and her mother is the Titan Leto, or according to some, Demeter.

She is sometimes called the Virgin Huntress, which may have simply meant she is chaste, or possibly an earlier meaning: an independent woman, beholden to no man. She is often depicted as a tall, slender maiden wearing a short, white tunic. She races through the forest with her nymphs and hounds, carrying a silver bow and a quiver of arrows. Though she certainly hunts animals, she also protects the young creatures of the woods. Her symbols include the crescent moon, the stag, the cypress, and of course the bow and arrow. When the moon first appears as a slim crescent, low on the western horizon, it is called "Diana's Bow."

She protects mothers, and women in general, and some of her rites celebrated women's mysteries and rites of passage: childbirth (she helped deliver Apollo), puberty, and motherhood.

She is honored by many titles: Artemis Agrotera (Artemis of the Mildland, patron of hunters), Potnia Theron (Mistress of Animals), Kourotrophos (Nurse of Youths), Phoebe (The Sun), and Locheia (Goddess of Childbirth and Midwives).

She has been conflated with many goddesses, including Diana, Hekate, Caryatis, and EILEITHYIA.

Artemis will be there for any child, especially girls, or woman who needs her; to help with passage through puberty; for issues of fertility, or to help in childbirth; to ward off contagious diseases; for sports injuries; for mental distress; and to help you find healing in nature. She will inspire you to a focused, swift, and relentless pursuit of peak health and fitness.

Artemis is the protector of small children

Asclepius: medicine, healing, rejuvenation

Asklēpiós, Aesculapius

Mediterranean, Greek

Asclepius is a deified mortal who became the god of medicine, healing, and rejuvenation, honored by physicians, nurses, and healers of many kinds.

He is a son of APOLLO and the mortal Coronis, and was raised and trained in medicine by the centaur physician CHIRON. His education was augmented by a snake whom Asclepius befriended; the snake (a symbol to the Greeks of wisdom, rebirth, and healing) licked his ears clean and whispered secrets of medicine and healing known only to the reptile tribe.

Asclepius became so proficient and powerful that he could bring patients back to life from the edge of death, and even resurrect the dead.

And Zeus killed him. Some say it was because Asclepius returned Hippolytus from the dead, and accepted payment for doing so. (In some ancient traditions, healing was thought to be a gift of the gods, and physicians' services were tainted if money changed hands.) Others suggest that Zeus' brother Hades was alarmed in case no more mortals would enter his underworld realm, or that Zeus thought humans would overpopulate the world if Asclepius saved them all.

The murder of his son infuriated Apollo, and to keep peace Zeus made Asclepius a god; or, according to legend, placed him in the night sky as the constellation Ophiuchus, the Serpent Holder. Images show him with a rod, wreathed with a single snake, which is still a symbol of medicine today. It is called the Rod of Asclepius, though other deities had similar rods.

Many famous healing temples, called Asclepieia, were scattered around the Mediterranean. The ill and injured came great distances to be healed by the priestesses and priests. Here, sacred serpents—the Aesculapian Snakes (the non-venomous *Zamenis longissimus*)—roamed freely. Supplicants would undergo ritual purification, make offerings to the god, then sleep in the temple sanctuary. Their dreams would be interpreted by priests or priestesses, who then prescribed treatment. This might include herbal medicines, ritual, or even having wounds licked by sacred dogs residing at the temple. Dogs are sacred to Asclepius.

Asclepius is associated with the Roman/Etruscan god VEJOVIS, the god ESHMUN, and the deified Egyptian polymath Imhotep.

He had several daughters and sons with his wife Epione, all of whom developed great skills in medicine and healing:

Epione (Soothing): a goddess who alleviates pain.

Aceso: a goddess who cures illness and heals injuries.

Aegle or Aglaea: goddess of radiant good health, adornment, beauty, and magnificence. Her name means "Brightness," or "Splendor." Her mother may have been the sun goddess Lampetia, rather than Epione.

Iaso or Ieso: goddess of modes of healing, medicine and remedies, and recuperation from illness. A mother herself, she oversees safe and healthy birthing.

HYGIEIA: goddess of cleanliness, sanitation, and health. Her skill and fame grew to match her father's (see HYGIEIA).

Panacea: goddess of the "universal remedy," a potion capable of curing any illness.

Machaon: a master surgeon who, in his spare time, shared the throne of a realm called Tricca.

Podaleirios: the other co-king of Tricca, particularly skilled in diagnostics.

Telesphoros: god of convalescence or recovery from injury and illness, who often accompanied Hygieia as she traveled the world.

Asclepius and his family make a formidable healing team, and can be invoked when a health crisis demands the most skilled help possible, and demands it now. Also, if your professional medical team comprises several different specialists who must coordinate their efforts, then Asclepius and his family may be the divine physicians who can make that happen.

Section II, Part 1

Babalú-Ayé: infectious diseases, epidemics

Anyigbato, Asojano, Obaluaiê, Palo, Shopona, Sagbata
Africa: Yoruba, Fon, Ewe; and the Caribbean and Latin America: Santeria, Candomblé, Umbanda and Macumba

Babalú-Ayé is an *orisha* of all infectious disease (including ebola and HIV/AIDS), epidemics, plague, pestilence, leprosy, influenza, and smallpox; and the healing of them all.

He is also associated with the Earth and the ancestors; the body; wealth and physical possessions; the cycle of life, death, and resurrection; righteousness, judgment, and punishment; roads, exile, movement, and displaced peoples; the permeable nature of things, symbolized by holes; secrecy and revelation; and the forest with its medicinal herbs and *ijimere* (spirits of the forest). Wow!

His name means Father, Lord of the Earth, and he is both feared for his ability to punish transgressors with disease, and venerated for his curative powers. His name is not spoken aloud, to avoid bringing disease, yet, as Shopona, he is thanked when he claims a victim. He is feared, loved, and respected.

He is shown as a lame old man, his face scarred by disease, who wanders the night in sackcloth and rattling snail shells. Often he wears a raffia costume that covers his whole body. He speaks to his followers through divination with cowrie shells, and December 17 is his special day of pilgrimage. His ritual tools include a broom for purification, a terra-cotta vessel with holes in the lid, and both cowrie and snail shells. He accepts grain as an offering, and dogs are his devoted companions.

According to myth, Nana Burukú may have been his birth mother, yet she left him on a beach to die of exposure. The infant was terribly scarred by voracious crabs. The goddess Yemaya found him and took him to her home, where she raised him and taught him many mysteries.

He was once exiled by Obatala (father god and the creator of human bodies), but he later returned to the community of orishas. Or not—some say he is still exiled.

Babalú-Ayé is no paragon of beauty and health; he is a complex and liminal figure, the Wounded Healer who lives with pain and disability, yet protects from disease, and heals the stricken. His journey includes exile and suffering, healing and restoration. Call him if your path has been very difficult, and especially if you are afflicted by serious and contagious disease. Speak not his name aloud, but show compassion to yourself, to him, and to others.

Section II, Part 1

Beiwe: fertility, mental and emotional health, SAD

Paive

Northern Europe, Sámi

Beiwe is a goddess of the sun, spring, renewal, and fertility of plants and animals. In her healing aspect, she gives the blessings of mental and emotional health; she is especially strong in curing people suffering from the cold and darkness of winter—what we would call Seasonal Affective Disorder, in its extreme form.

The Sámi are a traditional people of far northern Europe, whose culture is centered on the herding of reindeer. Their original religion is diverse across tribes, but includes animism, pantheism, polytheism, and shamanic practices. It is very deeply connected to the land they inhabit and to nature in general, with sacred sites at mountains and springs.

You might connect with Beiwe through drumming, chanting, and being in a meditative state while walking a labyrinth. Stone inscriptions called petroglyphs are part of the Sámi heritage. You could create a Beiwe shrine or talisman using her symbols: white female animals, especially reindeer; butter; and the color green.

If you wish to invoke Beiwe's help and consult a Sámi practitioner, know that some consider themselves to be authentic shamans or *noaidi* who work to reconstruct and continue indigenous traditions, while other "wise ones" offer their clients a mix of folklore, shamanic customs, and Christian elements.

You will want her by your side if you struggle with Seasonal Affective Disorder, or depression, or mental or emotional distress of any kind. Speak to her about fertility challenges, and honor her in the bright sunlight when you can.

Bona Dea: fertility, healing, regeneration, protector of abused women, herbal medicines

Mediterranean, Roman

Bona Dea is a goddess of fertility, abundance, healing, regeneration, and women (especially abused women), and also chastity and virginity. In early times, she was a goddess of the Earth (she could prevent earthquakes) and agriculture. Many saw her as a very personal savior, but she was also a protector of the people and state of Rome, and the Vestal Virgins presided over her rites in the capital.

Her name, or rather pseudonym, means simply Good Goddess in Latin, although she was honored with titles such as Augusta (Majestic), Domina (Lady or Mistress), Feminea Dea (The Women's Goddess), Sancta (The Holy One), Regina Triumphalis (Triumphal Queen), and Terrae Marisque Dominatrici (Mistress of Sea and Land).

Some identify her as the women's goddess Damia; or an earth goddess such as Ceres, Diana, Maia, Silvanus, or Terra; or Magna Mater, Fatua, or Ops. Her true name, however, was a closely guarded mystery.

Images show her as a dignified Roman matron, enthroned, holding a cup or bowl in her right hand; a snake is coiled around her arm and drinks from the cup. In her left arm she holds a cornucopia. The combination of serpent and cornucopia is unique to Bona Dea.

She was possibly the wife or daughter of Faunus, who abused her; so she is also identified with Fauna, a goddess of nature who could foretell the fates of women.

Her devotees included all classes, from slaves and freedmen to the most elite aristocrats. Though she is primarily a goddess of women, many men made offerings to her as well.

She was honored at two major festivals each year, open only to women and held at night. Both doubtless included dancing, wine, music, sacrifices of suckling pigs, and offerings of flowers and milk. The first event occurred at Bona Dea's principal temple, on the Aventine hill in Rome, on the May 1st anniversary of its founding, and seems to have been a mystery rite. It was attended by women of all classes, especially in the Republican era.

In December, gatherings were held in the private homes of Roman magistrates, and attended by women of the wealthy and privileged upper classes. All males (even male pets and portraits) were ushered out, and the home was decorated with greenery and blossoming flowers. A statue of Bona Dea and an image of a snake were placed on a couch as honored guests. Female musicians serenaded the feasting participants. It was a celebration of femaleness, independent of any male perspective or influence.

Bona Dea's principal temple was walled, presumably to discourage prying eyes or visitors. It was an important healing venue, where, (as with the temples to ASCLEPIUS), snakes roamed the chambers and priestesses dispensed herbal medicines. Her provincial temples and sanctuaries follow the same pattern.

Though she has a special concern for women's well-being, and particularly women who have suffered abuse, she also hears the pleas of men of honor. She can make herbal medicines and natural remedies more potent, and supports abundant health and prosperity.

Borvo: healing waters, medicinal potions

Borbanus, Borbetomagus, Bormanicus, Bormanus, Bormo, Boruoboendua, Borus, Labbonus, Vabusoa

Europe, Celtic: Lusitania (western Iberian Peninsula)

Borvo is a healing god of rivers, fountains, and minerals, especially associated with bubbling spring water. His worship was common in France, Spain, Portugal, and the Netherlands, at the very least.

His name is apparently based on the root *boru-, variously translated as boiling, bubbling, effervescing, cooking, or seething; and related to the Sanskrit word for violent or passionate, and the English word brew. The name of the River Barrow (Boiling) in Ireland comes from the same root.

He seems to have no symbols except bubbling springs.

Borvo had a divine consort, listed as the goddess Damona in several inscriptions, although in others his wife was named as Bormana. His companion is occasionally Candidus, the "candid spirit." Some myths mention him with a male friend, Macusanus or Baldruus, a kind of Celtic version of HERAKLES.

He is equated with APOLLO in many areas, although interestingly with the war god Mars in Portugal.

Borvo is an excellent spirit to have with you if your health regimen includes the healing properties of thermal springs, hot tubs, spas, or the therapeutic technique called *watsu*, and he could also enhance the effects of medicinal potions and brews. His association with Mars, and his Herakles-like companions, suggest that he could boost your strength, energy, and will to live.

Brigit: fertility, childbirth, eyes, leprosy, healing wells and springs, magick, healer of animals

Braga, Bragança, Bregenz, Breo Saighead, Brid, Bride, Bridget, Brigantia, Brigantis, Brìghde, Brighid, Brighit, Brigid, Brigindo, Brigin-Do, Brigindū, Ffraid

Europe, Celtic: Ireland to Austria

Brigit is a great goddess of fertility, childbirth, healing, healing wells and springs, eye afflictions, leprosy, the coming of spring, fire, the sun, women, hearth and home, domestic animals, inspiration, poetry, crafts, smithcraft, magick, divination, prophecy, serpents (in Scotland), and battle (as Brigantia).

Her name probably derives from Celtic *brig*, Exalted One or High One. She is the goddess of all things lofty, whether physical (towers, hill-forts, mountains, and highlands) or psychological (wisdom, druidic lore, high intelligence, eloquence, fine craftsmanship, and general excellence). Brigit was id the patron of healers and magicians, poets and bards, and artisans of all kinds.

She is one of the ancient and mysterious Tuatha Dé Danann, the daughter of the Dagda and had four half-siblings. The healing goddess had two full sisters, also named Brigit but with different specialties; so in many traditions she is venerated as a triple goddess of healing, inspiration, and smithcraft.

She married the god Bres, and they had a son named Ruadán. When he was killed, Brigit was the first to practice keening, a wailing lament for the dead.

As an ancient Celtic goddess, she had a sanctuary at Kildare, Ireland, where nineteen priestesses kept an eternal flame burning in her honor, within a sacred hedge that no man was allowed to cross. (Brigit herself tended the flame on every twentieth day.) Later it was said that the Christian Saint Brigid founded an abbey there. The goddess may have been simply adopted as a saint by the early Christian church, or St. Brigid may have been a historical human woman, perhaps named for the goddess. If there were two entities, one divine and one mortal, their mythologies have become completely intertwined.

Her special feast day, both as goddess and saint, is February 2, or February Eve (the evening of February 1 through the next day). It has many names: Imbolg or Imbolc (in the belly), Oimelc (ewe's milk), the Feast of Flames, La Fheill Bhride, and, for Christians, Candlemas. It was originally a festival of the birthing of lambs, but also fire, purification, initiation, and the welcoming of spring. To celebrate, young people go door to door, begging alms (money or food) in her name. At home, the family makes a special bed for Brigit by the hearth, and might weave Brigit's Crosses from straw.

She is further honored at her many sacred wells across Ireland and beyond, by "well-dressing" or decorating the wells. Ribbons or cloth strips, called clooties, are tied to nearby trees or bushes as offerings and to ask her aid.

Brigit is a goddess of Fire and Water, passionate and caring, strong, practical, resourceful, and tenacious. Call upon her for help in childbirth (or questions of fertility), for sore or infected eyes, leprosy or other dread diseases, cleansing and purification, or if your animals are sick or hurt. She will reignite your inner fire and help you heal.

Section II, Part 1

Carna: physical and spiritual health, internal organs, digestion, well-being

Carda, Cardea, Cranê, Cranea

Mediterranean, Roman

Carna is a goddess (or possibly two, conflated) of physical and spiritual health, the internal organs (heart, lungs, and liver), digestion, well-being, wholeness, kinship, family life, change, opportunity, and the thresholds and door hardware that symbolize the home. She is human physicality, the body itself. In her distant past, she may also have been a goddess of the Earth and the moon.

Her name comes from *caro* or *carnis*, meaning flesh, meat, food. The word "incarnate" means "in the body."

Her feast day was June 1st, the *Kalendae Febrariae*, or *Bean-Kalends*, since it occurred at the time of the bean harvest. Bean dishes were sacred to her.

Carna could protect people and animals from the dreaded *striges*. These are winged demons, something like a cross between Harpies and shrieking, vampiric owls that suck blood from sleeping babies or other small creatures. They have bulging eyes, large heads, and sharp talons. Charms fixed on doorways, especially a whitethorn twig dedicated to Carna, will help repel these *striges*, and probably nightmares and other perils of the night as well.

Carna/Cardea can support any kind of physical help your body needs, and in particular the health and healing of your heart and other internal organs, as well as digestive issues. In addition to your other work with her, put a protective amulet or talisman of whitethorn at your doorway.

Featured Gods and Goddesses

Chinese Deities of Health and Healing

Chinese mythology includes so many healing gods and goddesses that including them all would exceed the scope of this book. However, these are some names and specialties for you to begin with, and you may wish to do further research.

GENERAL GODS OF HEALING:

    Wu Ben, also called Baosheng Dadi, god of medicine

    Wong Tai Sin, god with the power of healing

SPECIALIZED GODS OF HEALING:

    Shennong, mythical emperor who spread knowledge of herbs and medicine.

    Hua Tuo, god of surgery

    Sun Simiao, god of internal medicine, and Medicine King

    Wang Wei, god of acupuncture

    Li Shizhen, god of herbal medicine

    Tàiyī Zhǔshén, god of qi

    Táokāng Gěyán, god of essence

HEALING GODS AMONG THE EIGHT IMMORTALS:

    Zhang Guolao, whose wine has healing properties

    He Xiangu, whose lotus flower heals mental and physical ailments

    Li Tieguai, who alleviates the suffering of the poor, sick, and needy with special medicine from his gourd

THE MEDICINE KINGS:

    Pian Que, Medicine God-King

Wei Chizhuang	Wei Gudao
Wei Shanjun	Pi Tong

    Sun Simiao, Medicine King and god of internal medicine

Section II, Part 1

THE GODS OF THE NINE CHAMBERS (organs):

Jiànggōng Zhenren (heart)

Dānyuángōng Zhenren (kidneys)

Lántáigōng Zhenren (liver)

Shàngshūgōng Zhenren (lungs)

Huángtínggōng Zhenren (spleen)

Tiānlínggōng Zhenren (gall bladder)

Xuánlínggōng Zhenren (small intestine)

Wèijìngōng Zhenren (large intestine)

Yùfánggōng Zhenren (bladder)

THE GODS OF HYGIENE/CLEANLINESS/SANITATION:

Língbǎo Huǎnzhàosī Língguān

Yùqīng Tōngbiàn Shèmó Hīnghuì Língguān

Dāntiān Jiǔfèng Pòhuì Língguān

Wǔfāng Wǔdì Xièhuì Xiānguān

Tiānhé Dōngjǐngjūn	Chúhuì Shénjūn
Yuànzhào Fūren	Duànhuì Shénjūn
Jiǔtiān Yùnhuì Shénjūn	Mièhuì Shénjūn
Jiǔtiān Xièhuì Shénjūn	Xǐhuì Shénjūn
Shōuhuì Shénjūn	Dànghuì Shénjūn
Quèhuì Shénjūn	

The Chinese have a long and rich history, and have had ample time to develop healing philosophies and techniques that are very different from those used in the West, yet have served their people well for millennia. If you are having trouble healing with Western medicine—surgery and drugs—it might be worth your while to explore whether Chinese medicine can help you. If you do, ask the Chinese deities to guide your choices, perhaps through divination.

Featured Gods and Goddesses

Chiron: general healing, teacher of healers

Cheiron, Kheiron

Mediterranean, Greek

Chiron (Hand) is a centaur known for his knowledge and skill in healing, medicine, music, archery, hunting, astrology, and prophecy. He is the superlative centaur amongst his brethren, and the only one whose front legs are human, rather than equine. Chiron is notable in Greek mythology for nurturing youth.

His skills tend to match those of APOLLO, his foster father; and ARTEMIS, Apollo's sister, who helped raise him. His parents were the Titan Cronus who had taken the form of a horse and impregnated the nymph Philyra. Other centaurs were born of the sun and rainclouds.

Although a centaur, his status and heritage are shown by his human front legs. This difference may be due to Chiron's unique lineage, being the son of Cronus rather than of the sun and clouds. Chiron is often shown carrying a branch with dead hares he has caught hanging from it, and wearing clothes, demonstrating that he is more civilized than most centaurs.

In many Roman depictions of Chiron, he teaches Achilles the lyre, and here Chiron has a fully equine lower body, with ears of a satyr, folded over at the top. In more modern art, Chiron has retained an element of clothing and gained a laurel wreath, showing nobility or divinity, more consistent with the Greek view.

In both the Greek and Roman versions, he is the wise and gentle teacher, the instructor of the arts of healing and music, and was intelligent, civilized, and kind. His pupils included the mortal ASCLEPIUS, who was later deified for his healing powers.

According to myth, Chiron was hit in the thigh by a poisoned arrow. As master of the healing arts, he tried to use herbs to heal himself, but was unsuccessful. He died after nine days, and rose to the stars to become the constellation Centaurus. However, Zeus promised that as long as Chiron was needed as a teacher of demigods, he will exist in this world. He lives on today as a constellation and an inspiration.

Given his kind nature, he brings his considerable skills to assist anyone in need. Since his name means "hand," Chiron might be an appropriate patron for chiropractors, those who practice therapeutic massage, and practitioners of "hands-on" healing disciplines. He also reminds us of the healing power of music.

Dhanvantari: Ayurvedic medicine, blood disorders, herbs

Asia: India, Hindu

An avatar of Vishnu, Dhanvantari is the physician of the gods, and god of Ayurvedic medicine, the traditional healing regimen of India. He is a god of blood disorders and herbal medicine. He has four hands; with one he carries Amrita, the ambrosia of the gods, and with another he holds a leech. (Leeches were used by many ancient doctors as a painless form of bloodletting, which was thought to help patients regain their health.)

The handsome Dhanvantari emerged eons ago from the Ocean of Milk. His birthday is celebrated by the practitioners of Ayurveda every year in the autumn, on Dhanteras, two days before Diwali, the Hindu Festival of Lights.

Many temples are dedicated to Dhanvantari, and he is worshipped daily. In front of one temple there is an engraved stone, believed to be from the 12th century. According to the inscription, the statue within the temple was provided by Garuda Vahana Bhattar, a great ayurvedic physician. A healthful herbal decoction is given to visitors.

Call on Dhanvantari if you plan to use ayurvedic medicine, or have a blood disorder, or if you intend to support your health with any herbal potion or health beverage. He would probably approve of "green drinks," fruit smoothies, and green tea; anything that keeps you hydrated and provides essential vitamins and nutrients. Drink them regularly with ceremony and intention, while asking Dhanvantari to increase their potency.

Section II, Part 1

Dian Cécht: medicine, battle wounds

Cainte, Canta, Dia'necht, Diancecht, Dianchecht
Europe, Celtic: Ireland

Dian Cécht is a god of medicine and Chief Physician of the Tuatha Dé Danann. His son, Miach, was also a brilliant surgeon, and his daughter AIRMED was an herbal healer and magician.

They blessed a well called Slane, or Sláine, the Well of Health, which would heal any wound, even death (but not decapitation). Tuatha warriors, wounded in battle, could bathe there; they were healed, and continued fighting. At the second battle of Moytura, however, their enemies filled the well with stones, preventing the healings, and the well became known as the Heapstown Cairn.

Dian Cécht saved Ireland from dangerous serpents, and was indirectly the cause of the name of the River Barrow: The Morrigan bore a son of a "terrible aspect," and Dian Cécht, foreseeing danger, counseled that he should be killed to save the people. After its death, Dian Cécht opened the infant's heart, and found three serpents, which could have depopulated Ireland when they grew to full size. He killed them, burned them, and threw the ashes into a nearby river. They were so venomous that the river boiled, and all living things within it were killed, and the river has been called the Barrow (Boiling) ever since.

Once, Nuada, the King of the Tuatha Dé Danann, was seriously injured in battle when his arm was slashed from his body. Dian Cécht was immediately called, and he brought Airmid and Miach with him to assist. While Dian Cécht was working upon Nuada, it became increasingly clear that Airmid's and Miach's skills as healers were much greater than those of their father. Dian Cécht had decided to replace Nuada's severed arm with one that he had made from silver, but Airmid was able to regenerate the King's own arm perfectly. Then Miach, the surgeon, reattached it to the King's body. (According to the laws of the Tuatha Dé Danann, no one could ever be king unless his body was whole. If Nuada's own arm had not been re-attached to his body, then his reign as King would have ended.)

Dian Cécht, envious of Miach's superior skill, went into a towering rage. He drew his sword and three times struck Miach, with apparently mortal wounds; yet each time Miach healed himself. Finally, Dian Cécht severed Miach's brain from his skull, and he finally died of a wound he could not heal. (See AIRMED for the epilogue.) Suffice it to say, Dian Cécht took the life of his son and destroyed the work of his daughter.

Dian Cécht could hardly be left out of any list of divine healers; his skill was undeniable. Yet you might wonder why anyone would choose to work with him, given his ego and jealous rages. Many mortals also have fits of anger, during which they hurt those closest to them; these may stem from childhood abuse, or emotional illness, or even brain tumors. If it is wise to be wary of Dian Cécht, nonetheless we may learn from his tragic example. Do you experience destructive rage, or know someone who does? Then it's time for intervention before further damage is done.

Section II, Part 1

Ebisu: children's health, workplace injuries, bones

Hirugo, Hiruko, Kotoshiro-nushi-no-kami, Yebishu
Asia: Japan, Buddhist

The only one of Japan's Seven Lucky Gods to originate purely from Japan without any Hindu or Chinese influence, Ebisu rules children's health, the sun, good luck, fishermen, and workingmen.

He is known as The Laughing God, or Ebisu-Shark.

Ebisu probably first arose as a god of fishermen. Later, after his worship spread to merchants and others, his story became conflated with that of Hiruko, a child born without bones (or, in some stories, without arms and legs) because his mother did not perform her part of the marriage ceremony correctly. Hiruko struggled to survive, but was cast to the sea in a boat of reeds before his third birthday. He washed ashore and was cared for by the Ainu, aboriginal people of Hokkaido Island. Over time he grew legs and bones, and became the god Ebisu.

He is slightly crippled and deaf, but cheerful and auspicious nonetheless (hence his title). He is often shown wearing a tall hat, holding a rod and a large red sea bream or sea bass. He was often connected to whales and whale sharks because they bring lots of fish, and protect fishermen. Jellyfish are also associated with him. The *fugu* restaurants of Japan will often honor Ebisu.

Featured Gods and Goddesses

Ebisu is frequently paired with Daikokuten, another of the Seven Gods of Fortune, in displays by small shopkeepers. In some versions of the myth they are father and son (or master and apprentice). With Fukurokuju, they are known as the Three Gods of Good Fortune.

Ebisu's festival is celebrated on the twentieth day of the tenth month, when he alone of all the gods does not go to the Grand Shrine of Izumo, and so is available for worship.

Ebisu is the namesake for Yebisu beer, which was first brewed in 1890, and is currently brewed by Sapporo Brewery.

Ask Ebisu for help healing children's illness or injuries, or if you were injured on the job—especially if you are a fisherman or working on or near the sea. Health problems related to bones or legs are also a specialty for this strong, capable, and cheerful god.

Eileithyia: fertility, childbirth, midwives, children

Artemis Eileithyia, Eleutho, Ilithyia, or as the plural, Eileithyiai
Mediterranean: Greece, Crete

Eileithyia (Fluid of Generation, or The Bringer) is a goddess (or two) of childbirth, midwives, children, fertility, and creativity; midwife of the gods. Possibly originally two goddesses, one for difficult births, the other for easy deliveries.

She was a daughter of Hera, possibly by Zeus. Vases illustrating the birth of Athena from Zeus' head often show two assisting Eileithyiai, with their hands raised.

Women would call on her during childbirth:

When racked with labour pangs, and sore distressed
the sex invoke thee, as the soul's sure rest;
for thou Eileithyia alone canst give relief to pain,
which art attempts to ease, but tries in vain.
Artemis Eileithyia, venerable power,
who bringest relief in labour's dreadful hour.
—Orphic Hymn 2, to Prothyraeia, translated by Thomas Taylor, 1792.

Votive offerings to her have been found from Neolithic times through Minoan–Mycenaean times, with a revival in the Roman period. In Greek shrines, small terracotta votive figures depicted an immortal nurse who took care of divine infants.

Eileithyia, like Artemis and Persephone, is often shown carrying torches to bring children out of darkness and into light. Her Roman counterpart is Lucina (Of the Light); the Egyptian is TAWARET. Torches, white flowers, and music were sacred to her. She was born in a cave, and caves are sacred to her, for their resemblance to the birth canal.

Eir: medical skill, childbirth, children, epidemics

Eil, Eira, Eria, Eyr, Eyra
Scandinavia, Norse, Teutonic

Eir (Help, or Mercy) is a youthful goddess of healing, medical skill, childbirth, shelter, and protection, especially from epidemic disease; and physician to the gods. She may be an aspect of Frigg.

Eir taught medicine to women in ancient Scandinavia (women were the only physicians in this culture), and she has nine assistants. They all live on Lyfjaberg, the Hill of Healing. Legend says that any woman who could climb the hill to reach them would be cured of all ills. Eir can be seen as the Norse HYGIEIA.

She is called The Caring One, or Best of Physicians. Fulla, goddess of the fruitful Earth, is her sister.

She may be one of the Norns who shape the lives of children, or possibly one of the guardian spirits, who are said to shelter and save those who make offerings to them. They could be similar to protective spirits of the house, guarding both men and women.

Eir held power over life and death, and could decree either for any given individual. She was honored as a source of life from the humblest cottage to the courts of royalty.

If disease is epidemic across the land and you fear contagion, call upon her. If you are pregnant, she and her skilled assistants will be present as you give birth to new life. If you need a better home for the sake of your children's health and safety, she can lead you to shelter. She also reminds us that healing is hard work, and comes to those who are brave and tenacious.

Section II, Part 1

Endovelicus: health, safety, healing waters, dreams

Europe: Lusitania (western Iberian Peninsula)

Endovelicus (Very Good) is a major Iron Age solar god, patron of public health and safety, healing, dreams, and cthonic oracles. Endovelicus also protected cities or regions that venerated him.

After the Roman invasion, his cult spread to most of the Roman Empire, and people from all walks of life venerated him. The cult of Endovelicus prevailed until the 5th century, just when Christianity was spreading in the region.

One of his temples has an ancient sacred fountain, whose waters are still said to be medicinal. Inside the temple, steam would rise from the ground into the temple's chamber, and it was thought to give visions, much like the Delphi oracle of APOLLO. After receiving certain rites, if a person or priest slept in his sanctuary, Endovelicus would talk to them in their dreams, and even tell them about their own future or offer advice.

Sinks made in rocks have been found in his temples, suggesting ceremonies were held there, probably animal sacrifice (perhaps pigs), and, possibly, ritual feasts.

Endovelicus can help you if water therapy, including moisturizing steam, is part of your healing strategy. He can also give you healing guidance in your dreams if asked. If you are a professional dealing with public health, you will want this god as your patron; he can see the big picture and help you plan.

Erinle: patron of LGBT, herbs, bodily fluids

Inlé

Africa, Yoruba; and Latin America

Erinle is a spirit of abundance and healing, and a patron of gay people. He is a great hunter, herbalist, and farmer who became an *orisha* who protects the people of the town from invasions. His myth says that one day he sank into the earth near Ilobu and became a river.

His shrines contain smooth round stones from the Erinle River, a tributary of the Oshun River.

Ask Erinle to help you hunt down the resources you need for healing, whether that means the right medical professionals, knowledge, energy, or money to pay the bills. As a river spirit, he might be useful in any disease that relates to fluids: blood, hormones, etc. Get a smooth round river stone for your altar or to carry as a sacred object, to remind you that Erinle is always with you.

Erzulie/Erzulie Mapiangue: health, healing, sexuality, gay men, magick/deals with pain of childbirth, protector of the unborn and newborn

Erzili, Erzilie, Erzulie-Freda-Dahomey, Erzulie Mapiangue, Erzulie Vestery, Ezili Freda Daome, Grande Erzulie, Maitresse Erzulie, Maîtresse Mambo Erzulie Fréda Dahomey, and more

Caribbean, Haiti; Africa, Dahomey

Erzulie is extremely complex, so this is, of necessity, very superficial. She/they can be plural, a family of *loa, lwa,* or spirits in the Vodou faith. She has many aspects, including Erzulie Mapiangue, who deals with the pain of childbirth, and is protector of the unborn and newborns. Here we will focus on Erzulie Freda Dahomey, a *loa* of beauty, romantic love, sexuality, passion, health, healing, refinement, purity, cleanliness, abundance, luxury, fortune, prosperity, material success, the moon and night, dancing, perfumes, jewelry, flowers, luck in gambling, water, disorder, and reptiles. And still more, she is a powerful magician, a *Mambo* of great skill. She can be called the "Virgin of the Voodoo."

Erzulie Freda Dahomey is a study in contrasts. On one hand she is feminine, refined, coquettish, clean and fresh and fond of luxury, beauty, and fine clothes. She is elegant, compassionate and good-hearted. She is also flirtatious, seductive, and sometimes outrageous in her behavior. At the same time, she carries a deep sorrow, never quite able to have her heart's desire, to achieve the perfection she craves. She always ends a ritual in tears.

Erzulie also has darker aspects. She can be selfish, spoiled, vain, and lazy, and sometimes causes jealousy, discord, and the desire for vengeance.

She is reserved or even jealous toward women, and keeps her distance unless they are her daughters or *sevites* (servants or followers, sometimes priests or priestesses). She loves men, freely hugging and kissing them. She especially protects gay men.

She appears as a beautiful white woman, with long, blonde hair, wearing a pink gown and fine jewelry, including three gold wedding rings, for her three husbands. Or as a banana-eating water snake. Her symbols are a heart pierced with knives, and an elaborate *veve* (ritual drawing), at right. Her colors can be pink and white; pink, white, blue, and gold; or red, gold, and navy blue.

Thursday is the day sacred to Mambo Erzulie Freda, and the best time for a service or ritual. If you perform a ritual in service to Erzulie Freda, it must be done perfectly. She likes offerings of fine perfume, golden jewelry, scented soaps, frosted cakes and other rich foods, pink roses, cosmetics, and pink champagne. In certain rituals, she may possess the body of a participant, either female or male. This is a common phenomenon in Vodun ritual, and can be a very powerful spiritual experience.

Erzulie Freda is conflated with a *loa* named Metres Ezili, and the Virgin Mary as Mater Dolorosa (Our Lady of Sorrows).

Erzulie Freda is not a simple spirit, nor easy to work with. She demands cleanliness and refinement in her supplicants, and exacting attention to detail in her rituals. However, once motivated she has the power to accomplish anything she chooses—including great works of healing for those she cares for. In addition to physical cures, ask her to inspire you toward better self-care, and assertiveness in relationships that have not been supportive.

Section II, Part 1

Eshmun: healing, health, children, survivors of sexual abuse

Eshmoun, Esmoun, Esmun

Mediterranean: Phoenicia and others

Eshmun is a god of health and healing, especially of children, protector of those who have survived sexual abuse, and hunting. Eshmun can be seen as the Phoenician ASCLEPIUS.

Eshmun (The Eighth) was the eighth son of Sydyk.

The temple to Eshmun is found near the Phoenician port of Sidon on the modern River Awwali. Many votive offerings were found there, in the form of statues of persons healed by the god, especially babies and young children. Nearby is a gold plaque of Eshmun and the goddess HYGIEIA. In his right hand, Eshmun is holding a staff around which a serpent is entwined (this predates the Rod of ASCLEPIUS). A coin of the 3rd century CE from Beirut shows Eshmun standing between two serpents.

A very old underground temple called Eshmunit, with eight rooms (one large and seven small) carved into the bedrock and accessible by stairs, is in Bterram, a village in Lebanon. It may be a temple to a Eshmun, or to a spouse of his.

In his myth, the goddess Astronoë "so harassed him with amorous pursuit" that in desperation he castrated himself and died. Astronoë then warmed him with her body, restoring him to life, named him Paeon (Healer), and changed him into a god.

He is one of several healing deities who has a particular concern for children and babies, and he is a supportive healer for survivors of sexual abuse, since he experienced it and came back stronger than ever.

Fufluns: health, growth of all things, good cheer

Faflo, Faflond, Puphluns, Vertumnus

Mediterranean, Etruscan

Fufluns is a god of plant life, wine, happiness, health, and growth in all things; also a cthonic deity and psychopomp who guides souls to the underworld after death.

He is usually shown as a beardless youth, but is sometimes an older, bearded man.

Fufluns' myths parallel those of Dionysus, including the story of his birth. In myth, the pregnant Semla is killed by Tinia in the form of a lightning bolt; Tinia then sews the infant Fufluns into his thigh and later gives birth to him. However, in Fuflun's myth, his mother is either resurrected or immortalized, because she and an adult Fufluns are shown together in Etruscan artwork.

The myth of Fuflun and Areatha (the Etruscan Ariadne) follows the traditional Greek story, where Areatha helps Theseus escape the labyrinth of the Minotaur, but is then abandoned by him. Fufluns finds Areatha, falls in love with her, and they marry.

His Greek equivalent is Dionysus. The Romans meshed him with Bacchus, and his rituals were heavily influenced and changed under the influence of the Dionysian frenzies.

Illness or injury can bring not only pain and helplessness, but also self-pity and depression. Fufluns is a divine spirit who can lighten your mood and find things to enjoy and celebrate even in a difficult or terrible situation. Lift a glass of wine if you can, put on some great music, and resolve that whatever comes, you and the god will meet it with good cheer and courage.

Grannus: hot healing waters, diagnosis, the sun, sunburn, sunstroke

Amarcolitanus, Granus, Mogounus

Europe, Celtic: Gaul

Grannus is a god of spas, healing thermal and mineral springs, and the sun, sunburns, and sunstroke. He is associated with APOLLO as Apollo Grannus, a healing or solar deity, and with Phoebus as Apollo Grannus Phoebus (Bright, Shining, Radiant). He was frequently worshipped in conjunction with SIRONA, and sometimes with Mars and other deities.

Grannus is called Deus Apollo Grannus Amarcolitanus (The One with a Piercing or Far-Reaching Look). This may refer to his keen observation skills and diagnoses, or to his ability to see into the hearts of his many supplicants.

He had a prestigious healing center with hot springs at Aachen in Germany, once called Aquae Granni (The Waters of Grannus). There his annual festival lasted ten days and nights, and drew pilgrims from all over northern Europe.

Grannus is apparently particular regarding who will receive his healing largesse. The Roman Emperor Caracalla, a man of less than sterling reputation as a ruler, traveled to the shrine and made many rich offerings—but was denied healing because he was evil.

Grannus is a god who might be able to help find the diagnosis or source of a medical problem, if it has been elusive. If warm water soaks are valuable to you in relieving pain or promoting healing, ask him to boost their effect. If you suffer from burns or sunstroke, ask him to promote gentle healing of your skin. He is more likely to grant healing if you are caring and compassionate.

Gula: The Great Physician, creation, illness and good health, medicine, healing, fever, inflammation, fatigue, magick, and dreams

Baba, Bau, Gatamdug, Gula-Bau, Mah, Nin Ezen, Ninkarrak, Ninki, Nintinugga, Nm-din-dug

Mesopotamia: Sumer, Babylon, Assyria, Akkadia

Gula (The Great Physician, and The Lady Who Restores to Life) is a mother goddess of creation, illness, good health, vital heat, medicine, healing rituals and incantations, and protector of boundaries and homes. She lives in a beautiful garden at the center of everything, where she waters the tree that is the axis of the world. She picks the fruit of the tree to give to her followers.

She has a less benign side, though, since she curses subjects who disrespect the prerogatives of rulers, and punishes poisoners. (This may be the origin of the Old Testament's admonition, "Thou shalt not provide livelihood to a poisoner," mistranslated in the 16th century as "Thou shalt not suffer a witch to live.")

As Gatamdug, she interprets dreams. As Mah, she/he is androgynous, sometimes male, sometimes female. As Nintinugga, she was the daughter of An and the wife of Ninurta (also named Ninib or Ninip), a sun god of hunting and war. They had seven daughters.

She was known over a vast stretch of time in many cultures, under many names, sometimes working alone and sometimes with her consort, who was also known by many names. Perhaps this was one goddess who spread throughout the region and assumed new names, or maybe several different healing goddesses were conflated and blended into one.

Her image is frequently shown on Babylonian boundary marker stones, or *kudurru*, which depicted the gods who ratified the land grants, the contract or grant itself, and the consequences for violating the terms, which usually included a divine curse. The famous Kudurru of Gula shows her seated on a throne, wearing a long, multi-layered skirt and stepped headdress, with a companion dog beside her and images of the sun, moon, and a star above. Her primary symbol is the eight-rayed orb of vital heat, which can be the life-giving heat of the body, or the fever that can kill. She is also associated with the Tree of Life.

The Sumerians had their own myth of a Great Flood, in which most humans drowned. It was Gula who descended when the waters subsided, and breathed life back into humanity.

She had a temple in Babylon itself, another in Lagash, where she was the city's patron, plus shrines and chapels in other cities.

The proper position to assume when asking for her aid is to stand with both hands raised, like a tree. Call upon Gula to help abate fevers or inflammation; or in cases of fatigue, to heal and boost your energy field. She can also help you understand troubling dreams or nightmares, bring restful sleep, and help you maintain personal boundaries that will support your health.

Haumea: fertility, childbirth, death and rebirth

Faumea, Haumea tikitiki, Ka meha i kana, Nona
Oceania: Polynesia, Hawaii, New Zealand

Haumea is the goddess of fertility, childbirth, nature, wild and domesticated plants, disorder, weather, fire, tradition, death and rebirth, renewal, and immortality. Haumea's symbols are fresh flowers, *leis* (flower garlands), and local foods. Do not confuse the goddess with Haumia, a Maori god of wild foodstuffs.

Haumea is the Mother of Hawaii, and created its islands and all the living things upon them, including the Hawaiian people. She is the source and patron of Hawaiian culture and tradition. She is called Tree of Changing Leaves. Like some other goddesses, she can grow old and then renew herself at will, becoming a young woman as often as she pleases.

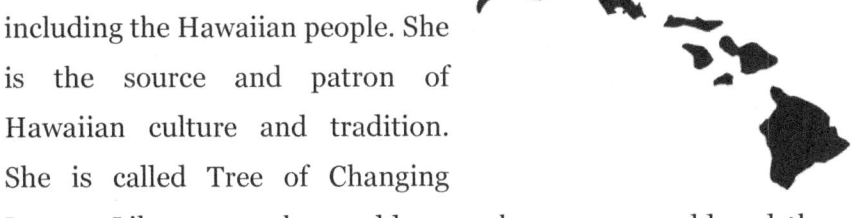

Most of the time she is a very generous and benevolent goddess, though when given cause, she can become angry, bringing famine or causing her daughter Pelé to erupt rivers of fiery lava, and bring destruction to villages below.

Haumea bore many living things, both animal and human. Most were born not in the usual way, but from several parts of her body. She is loving and sensual, and not reluctant to bestow her favors on any handsome young man, even her direct descendants.

One of her primary stories concerns the process of human childbirth. In ancient times, women were unable to give birth in the way we know today. Every pregnancy required a "C-section," and the mothers often died. But Haumea taught women the secret of giving birth naturally, and countless lives were saved.

How fascinating it is that one of the newly discovered dwarf planets in our solar system, far beyond the orbit of Neptune, was named for Haumea; its two satellites were named Hi'iaka and Namaka, for two of her daughters. The planetoid takes 285 Earth-years to circle the sun, but spins on its axis in only four hours... and it is the only known planet to be basically egg-shaped.

If you would like Haumea's help in healing from your illness or injury, bring her offerings of flowers and Hawaiian foods, such as *poi*, *kālua* pig, *laulau* (steamed mixed fish and meat), macadamia nuts, Kona coffee, and pineapple. Better yet, share the feast with her, and perhaps entertain her with singing and dancing. (She might also like a monetary offering to an organization that preserves traditional Hawaiian culture).

Heka: health, wellness, medicine, magick, the life force

Hike

Africa, Egyptian

Heka is a primal god of magick, medicine, health, and wellness. He might be said to be the divine personification of magick; the practice of ancient medicine was understood as one branch of magick, rather than a set of scientific and practical skills.

His name loosely means Magick, but more specifically *He Ka* is "the activation of the *ka*," or "action of the *ka*." The *ka* is one part, the vital force or life energy, of the complex Egyptian model of the soul. Magick was performed by activating and harnessing this power; strong when it was your own *ka*, but powerful beyond belief when the magician drew upon the divine *Ka* of the gods.

At the beginning of all things, "before duality had yet come into being," according to an ancient Egyptian text, Heka was created by Atum (the Egyptians' primary creator god); though other sources say his father was Khnum (the god of the source of the Nile) and his mother Menhit (a Nubian war goddess).

The myth of Heka tells that he once fought with two giant serpents, and overcame them; he is shown as a muscular hero choking the entwined snakes. Heka is expressed in hieroglyphics by a pair of raised arms with a twist of flax between them.

Heka is not simply magick in general, but particularly the power of the voice and the spoken word. Memorizing the correct spells and incantations could make the difference between entering a happy afterlife and losing your soul forever; certain sacred passwords were painted on the interior lids of coffins, so the soul could not lose or forget them.

Is there a link between the elder goddess Hekate, listed as a Greek Titaness but known to be older, and the Egyptian god Heka, or the goddess of midwifery Hekt? This is a mystery worth exploring, for anyone who wants to work with any of them.

If you lack energy and vitality, call upon Heka. And he reminds us that words have power; negative self-talk ("I'm a mess, I'm never gonna get better") can only block the healing the process, while positive words—such as affirmations or afformations—will enhance it.

Herakles: men's health, and their strength, fertility, and sexuality

Hercules

Mediterranean, Greek

Herakles is a divinely sired hero of health, strength, athletics, gymnasiums, and heroic deeds, patron to boys and young men, a noble example of proud masculinity. He is the gatekeeper and guardian of Olympus, a protector of mankind, slayer of monsters, and also god of agriculture, fertility, trade, and oracles.

He is the son of Zeus and Alcmene, a lovely princess of Argos, and foster son of her husband Amphitryon, who raised Herakles as his own. Like other divine Greeks, he was enthusiastically adopted by Rome. Roman emperors often promoted themselves as latter-day Hercules, to add luster to their reputations.

Legends often focus on his extraordinary strength and courage, but he is no thick-skulled muscleman. He used ingenuity and wits in crises, as when he tricked Atlas, or cleaned King Augeas' stables as one of his Twelve Labors. He is known as a loyal friend and a terrible enemy, passionate and strong in his feelings. A mighty lover with women and men alike, he has a gentle side, playing with children as easily as he might wrestle a wild lion.

He is usually shown wearing a lion skin and wielding a huge club. His popularity extended even to the British Isles; the Cerne Abbas Giant, carved 180 feet tall and 167 feet wide into a chalk hillside, is thought to be his likeness. Legend says that making love on the great phallus of the image brings fertility.

Men who have sexual issues, want to have children, or who need health, strength, and vitality will find Herakles a mighty ally.

Hygieia: health, especially cleanliness, hygiene, sanitation, prevention of illness and infection, preventive medicine, mental health, herbs

Hygeia, Hygiea

Mediterranean, Greek and Roman

Hygieia is the personification of health, cleanliness, hygiene, sanitation, and mental health. Unlike many goddesses and gods of healing, who acted after an injury occurred or illness developed, Hygieia's mission is to prevent accident, infection, and epidemics. Thus, she is a goddess of safety and preventive medicine.

She is a daughter of the famous healers ASCLEPIUS and Epione; her sisters and brothers were all healers as well.

Images and statues show her as a young woman with a large snake wrapped around her; often the serpent drinks from a bowl, cup, or jar that she holds (the goddess SIRONA was depicted in much the same way). Her brother Telesphorus, the god of convalescence and recovery, traveled with her. Hygieia's symbol is a bowl, cup or chalice with a snake twined around its stem, its head poised above it; along with the mortar and pestle used for grinding herbs, it is one of the traditional symbols of pharmacy.

The Romans conflated her with Valetudo, goddess of personal health, and Salus, goddess of public health and welfare. But before that, she was equated with Athena, as Athena Hygieia. Legend says that as the Parthenon was being built, a skilled workman had a terrible fall and was severely injured; the physicians held out no hope for him. But Athena Hygieia appeared in a dream to Pericles (a brilliant statesman and orator of Athens) and explained how to heal the victim. He followed her counsel and the man was healed.

In the fifth and third centuries BCE, plagues struck Athens and then Rome; one result was that veneration of Hygieia spread rapidly (and, hopefully, public sanitation measures followed).

Supplicants left hair clippings and articles of clothing on statues of her (much like clooties; see BRIGIT) as a way to direct the goddess' healing powers to them.

Call upon Hygieia when you want to change your lifestyle to include healthier habits and better personal hygiene; or when an epidemic occurs and you wish to protect yourself and your family. To ask her blessing, you might say: "Hygieia, most revered of the blessed gods, with thee may I dwell for the rest of my life, and may thou be a gracious guest of my house" (from the Hymn to Hygieia, by Ariphron, 4th cen. BCE); or address her as Licymnius did, "'Bright-eyed mother, highest queen of Apollon's golden throne, desirable, gently laughing Hygieia,' protect my health and the health of the ones I love."

Isis: sexuality, fertility, motherhood, children's illnesses, healing, magick, protector of the dead, reincarnation and rebirth, snakebite, massive injury

Aset, Au-Set, Eset, Tait, and many more
Africa, Egyptian

Isis is a goddess of magick, divination, healing, purification, initiation, protection of the dead, rebirth and reincarnation, womanhood, love, fertility, marriage, sexuality, motherhood, nature, spinning, weaving, metalwork, civilization, the arts, fate, and perfection, and she is the patroness of priestesses. She is the ideal wife and mother, and with her husband and son, part of a divine trinity. She is the Great Mother, Giver of Life.

Her name means Throne, and she is sometimes shown with a miniature throne symbol on her headdress, and holding a lotus. She is often shown with wings outstretched, but sometimes seated on a throne nursing Horus. Isis and the cow-goddess Hathor became blended at some point, and then she often wore the horns of a cow on her head, surrounding a crimson solar disc. Her chief symbols are the throne and the Buckle of Isis or Knot of Fate. She is called Queen of the Earth, Goddess of Life, Protectress of the Dead, Mother of the Seasons, and Queen of the Stars.

She is a daughter of Nuit, goddess of the sky and starry heavens, and Geb, the Earth God. She is the sister and wife of

Osiris and the mother of Horus, the falcon-headed god, and Bast, the cat-goddess. In ancient depictions, Isis is often paired with her faithful sister Nephthys, especially in funerary art.

Her central myth explains why she is considered a vastly powerful goddess of healing. Her brother Set was jealous of Osiris, and plotted to murder him. Set dismembered the body, and hid the pieces all over the world. So great was her love for Osiris, that she did not rest until she found the parts (except for one) and brought him back to life. They miraculously conceived Horus, and then Osiris retired to become lord of the underworld.

Another important myth tells us that Ra created the world through his magick, and that when Isis saw this, she desired to have the same arcane knowledge and skills. She devised a clever plan to have a serpent waylay Ra and bite him. Ra could not counteract the poison, but Isis, the great healer, offered to do so—for a price. She demanded that Ra reveal his True Name, the source of his magickal power... and thus his powers became hers as well. She healed him of the snakebite.

In ancient Egypt, she was honored with great festivals in the spring and fall, and one in June known as The Night of the Teardrop. Another, called The Festival of Lights, occurred the night of August 12, by torchlight.

Isis was once described as "the clever-tongued one whose speech never fails," which may indicate a connection to HEKA, the god of sacred words and magick.

Isis was the divine mother for all Egypt, and her following grew far beyond that, to Greece and even Rome. Many who sought the Divine Feminine found her—perfect. However, Roman aristocrats sneered at her worship; Emperor Augustus banned it during his reign in an attempt to reinvigorate the worship of Roman gods; the Christian Church outlawed it in the 6th century; and with the coming of Islam she was cast aside in her homeland…. yet she was never without those who honored her.

Today she is at the center of Egyptian reconstructionist (Kemetic) religion with Osiris and Horus, and is honored by many Wiccan groups (Dianic and otherwise), as well as by the far-flung Fellowship of Isis, headquartered in Ireland, and by many other Neopagans. She is a goddess both lasting and beloved.

Her powers seem to have no limits, so one might call upon her for any healing need, but recalling her feat with Osiris, perhaps especially for massive injury, including dismemberment. Also, considering her reputation as a loving mother, any illness or injury affecting children would doubtless stir her compassion.

Ixchel: sexual relations, women's fertility, childbirth, midwifery, medicine, general healing

Chibilias, Ix Chel, Ix-Chel, Ix Ch'up, Ix Hun Zipit Caan
Central America, Mayan

Ixchel is an elderly jaguar goddess of women's fertility, sexual relations, childbirth, midwifery, healing, weather, the moon, water, weaving, and the secrets of medicine. She is part of a gathering of midwife goddesses known as the "female lords." She may also preside over the sweat bath, where Mayan mothers liked to cleanse and relax before and after giving birth. She lives in the land of mists and rainbows. No one knows the meaning of her name; suggestions include The Red Goddess, Rainbow, Evening Star, or Woman with a Pale Face, perhaps referring to the moon.

She may have been seen as the waning moon, which is often called Our Grandmother. Ixchel corresponds fairly closely to the Aztec goddess Toci Yoalticitl: Our Grandmother, Physician of the Night. Ixchel is also sometimes represented as very similar to Aztec earth goddesses, and her jaguar nature might indicate that she is also a warrior. She seems to be a rain goddess as well; in one image, she empties a water jar to symbolize a downpour ejected by a heavenly dragon; this may represent a mythic, worldwide flood or simply the annual return of the rainy season.

She is shown as an ancient woman, sometimes with the ears of a jaguar, and eagle claws rather than hands. Her skirt flows with fertile waters, and water lilies are scattered upon it, or sometimes it has a pattern of crossed bones. Upon her head is a coiled serpent or a crown of feathers. Her symbols include turquoise; jade; anything silver, blue, or white; water; and a jar, either filled with rainwater, or upside down and empty. The inverted version may represent the rain poured out upon the land, or a womb that has just given birth to a child.

Ixchel is partnered with Itzamna, the creator god.

Her sacred places include a small island to the north of Cozumel, called by the Spanish explorers Isla Mujeres (the Island of Women). Mayan women would travel here in order to honor Ixchel and ask that their marriages be fruitful. Here, too, the festival Ihcil Ixchel was celebrated, especially by the *hechiceros* (shamans) and physicians. Sacred medicine bundles holding small images of Ixchel were displayed, and divination would be performed using special stones.

Women could call upon Ixchel for fertility, and those already pregnant may invoke her for a safe and easy birth. Since she holds all the secrets of medicine, she can assist with any healing, especially for women. Ask her presence when you slip into a cleansing hot tub, sweat lodge, sauna, or hot spring; and seek her fierce protection as a jaguar warrior, if you feel threatened.

Kumugwe: healing waters, general healing

Goomokwey, Komokwa

North America, Pacific Northwest: Nuxalk and Kwakwaka'wakw Nations

Kumugwe is the god of the seas, and especially the world beneath the waters. He has the power heal the sick and injured, and to know the future. He will give rich gifts and powers to those he favors, but can also manifest a fierce and terrifying aspect, even eating the eyes of those who anger him. He is master of those human souls whose lives are claimed by stormy seas or shipwreck.

Kumugwe is enormous, so big that his movements cause the ebb and flow of the tides; and on those rare occasions when he rises to the surface of the ocean, his huge head can be mistaken for an uncharted island. He is sometimes envisioned in the form of an octopus. In ceremonial masks, he is depicted with round fishlike eyes, fins, suction cups, rows of gills, and seabirds or fish upon his head. As one would expect, sea creatures are sacred to him, especially the seal, the octopus, sea lions, orcas, and loons.

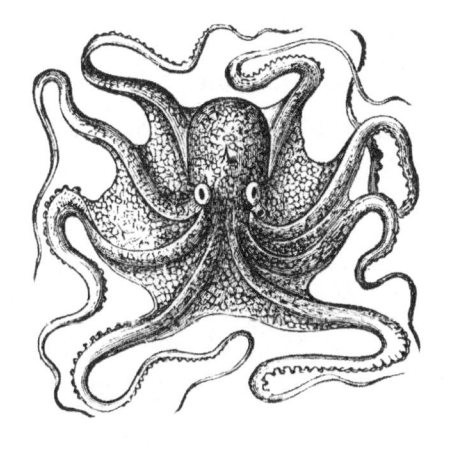

Kumugwe means Wealthy One, appropriate to one who is master of all the wealth in the sea, and the treasures among the jetsam and sea wrack cast on land by the waves.

His home, deep undersea, is vast and rich. We might imagine it as encrusted with pearls, branching corals, and rare shells in vibrant colors. Great sea lions stand like the caryatids on a Greek temple, living columns and pillars supporting the arching domes and spires. A large and powerful octopus guards this realm, its colors shifting to match the seabed as it patrols for intruders.

The classical hero's journey, in Pacific Northwest terms, has the bold warrior facing underwater perils in a quest to reach Kumugwe's deep home. Those who survived received gifts of copper, blankets, and ceremonial regalia. More importantly, they would be taught the lore, magick, and secrets of the sea, becoming powerful shamans and healers.

Call upon him for healing related to blood and the fluids of the body, as well as injuries sustained on the sea, or for deep emotional wounds.

If you love the oceans and beaches, you may discover a special link with Kumugwe; but you must also find the courage within your heart to approach him, for he can be as capricious as the sea, offering calm sunlit waters one day and raging storm winds the next. Yet he can teach you the deep rhythms and tides of the sea, and help you to swim with them. In your healing quest, you may not fight the ocean's power, but you may join with it.

Kupalo/Kupala: cleansing water, health, longevity, herbs, mental and emotional health, infection

Europe, Slavic: Bulgarian, Serbian, and Russian

Kupalo/Kupala (To Bathe) is a goddess of midsummer, fire, water and springs, cleansing, health, happiness, longevity, mental and emotional health, protection against infection, and herbs.

She is mistress of all the herbs, but her favorites are purple loosestrife (its roots are good for banishing bad dreams and demons, if gathered on summer solstice morning), and the flowering fern (which gives the ability to understand the trees). Her symbols are water, flowers, ferns, and birch wood.

In her rituals, a straw or birch effigy is made from a sapling with just the top leaves remaining, and dressed in women's clothing. A bonfire is lit, and young people jump it, holding the effigy. The next day they bathe with the effigy in a river or in the dew collected on Midsummer morning, then let it float away (if in the river), taking their illness and all evil away with her.

In Serbia and other Slavic countries, women seeking her help would hang an image of Kupalo, dressed in the best finery, from a sapling that just had its top leaves left after stripping.

Kupalo can help if you need to cleanse yourself of infection or negative thoughts and feelings. If you are using herbal medicines, call upon her expertise and power.

Kwan Yin: fertility, childbirth, health, healing, purification; compassion for grief, suffering, and despair

Guanyin, Kannon (for which the company Canon, Inc., is named), Kuannon, Quan Yin, and dozens more variations
Asia

Kwan Yin is a Goddess/bodhisattva of mercy, fertility, health, childbirth, healing, unconditional love and compassion, kindness, the relief of suffering, purification, and enlightenment, and song. She is protector of women and children, and a patroness of priestesses. She protects fishermen and all who are out on the sea; business people and traders; and travelers of all kinds. She is also seen as the protector of the unfortunate, all who are sick, disabled, poor, or in trouble. After the Great Flood, she sent down a dog holding rice grains in its tail, so she is worshiped as an agrarian and agriculture goddess, too. Kwan Yin is a Taoist Immortal.

She is known as the Goddess of Mercy, a compassionate goddess who hears the cries of sentient beings, and has miraculous powers to help those who call her. The Chinese name Guanyin is short for Guanshiyin, meaning [The One Who] Perceives the Sounds of the World, or She Who Hears the Weeping World.

As Avalokiteshwara in India, she is called The One with a Thousand Arms and Thousand Eyes. When she saw that there was suffering in the world, she reached out, but her arms shattered under the force of the suffering of the world. The Buddha Amitabha gave her eleven heads and a thousand arms, in order to better hear and help the suffering beings.

The Lotus Sutra says "it is easier to count all the leaves of every tree of every forest and all the grains of sand in the universe than to count the blessings and power of Avalokiteshwara."

East Asian followers believe that Kwan Yin originated as the Bodhisattva Avalokiteśvara. This is often considered the most beloved Buddhist Divinity, who can take the form of any type of God, Buddha, or king, any gender, adult or child, human or non-human being, in order to relieve the suffering of sentient beings.

Avalokiteśvara was originally depicted as a male bodhisattva, wearing chest-revealing clothing and a light moustache. In modern times, Kwan Yin is more often shown as a beautiful woman in white robes, looking down as she watches over the world. She usually wears necklaces symbolic of Indian or Chinese royalty. Her left hand holds a jar containing pure water, and the right holds a willow branch. In China, she is often shown standing atop a dragon, or with a white cockatoo and two children or two warriors. Her symbols are the lotus, black tea, rice, and rainbows.

Her story tells that as a human woman, she was executed at her father's orders. After willingly taking on all of the executioner's karma, she descended into hell. While she was there, she heard the suffering of the beings of the world, and compassionately released all her good karma to return the souls back to the Earth. She turned Hell into Paradise, and vowed never to return to Paradise until all suffering was gone from the Earth.

If your illness or injury has brought you to great sadness, grief, even despair, know that Kwan Yin will hear you and offer comfort. Though she shows special concern for women, babies, and children, her heart is open to the suffering of men as well. As one who transitioned from a male bodhisattva to a goddess, she has special empathy for transgender people. Rattles or fireworks are traditionally used to add emphasis to prayers to her. Remember that she teaches us that love and tenacity can transform even a hell into something beautiful.

同情　Compassion

Mama Cocha: healing water, healing, health, nutrition, stress and mental health

Cochamama, Mama-Qoca, Mama Qocha, Mama Qucha

South America: Peru, Inca, Chincha

Mama Cocha is goddess of the oceans, water, health, healing, fishing, and sea creatures; patron of sailors and fishermen; provides nutrition; relieves stress, and brings mental health. She is the living energy of water, source of health and the provider of food from the seas, especially whales. She blesses her people with an abundant supply of fish, and protects sailors by calming the waves when storms threaten. Her symbol is the whale, and she loves blue and green.

Her name means Mother Ocean or Sea Mother. She is the wife of the great creator god Viracocha (or Wiraqucha), and mother of the moon goddess Mama Quilla (or Killa) and the sun god Inti.

If you are serious about preserving your health through good nutrition, Mama Cocha can inspire you; what is healthier than fresh and untainted seafood? If you visit her at a large lake or the ocean, she can also cleanse negativity from your heart and mind, and calm dangerous stress and tension by attuning you to the long, slow, endless rhythms of the tides.

Section II, Part 1

Mami Wata: healing, health, fertility, sex, water

La Sirène, Mama Glow, Maman Dio, Mammy Water, River Maiden, Watermama, Watramama, and more

Africa, southeastern Nigeria, Efik, Ibibio and Annang people; Americas, Caribbean

Mami Wata (Pidgin English for Mother Water) is not one goddess, but a huge array of overlapping water deities associated with healing, fertility, sex, lust, and fidelity. Such spirits are female in most cases, but sometimes male. Water spirits have been well known in Africa since ancient times, since waterways provide so much that is essential to the communities near them. In general, these spirits are neither unequivocally good nor evil.

As with many healing deities, she can inflict illness or cure it: everything from barrenness to headaches fall under her power. As with health, so with water; she can cause flooding or drowning, or protect people from the perils of rivers and seas. Overall, she is regarded as a benevolent spirit, or spirits, more likely to give health and wealth than to withhold them.

In recent times, she is often depicted as a mermaid, with the lower part of a fish or serpent. Her hair is long and black, and may be kinky, curly, or straight. The indigenous tribes of Africa may have got the mermaid image from carved figureheads of European ships, or the tales of sailors.

In some stories, Mami Wata appears as an attractive woman, with a large snake coiled around her body, and its head between her breasts. In her human form, she wears expensive jewelry and is shown with a mirror and comb. But, having divine powers, she can also appear as a man, or in other guises.

Her shrines are decorated in red (for power, heat, maleness, destruction, and physicality) and white (for beauty, new life, femaleness, spirituality, and water), and are filled with offerings and sacrifices: incense, dolls, jewelry, bells, carvings, colorful prints, and images of women with children. Devotees wear red and white, and sometimes wear cloth snakes around the waist.

Myths tell us that she most often appears to solitary individuals, sometimes kidnaps people from their boats, or while they are swimming, and takes them to her ocean realm. If they are ever freed—not a certainty—they return spiritually changed in a subtle way, and may become successful and more attractive. Men encountering her may be seduced before discovering her true nature; they are required to swear fidelity to her alone, and to be silent about their relationship. The faithful are rewarded with great wealth, but the faithless are ruined.

People celebrate her by dancing and bringing offerings of jewelry, fragrant soaps and perfumes, and food and drink, from wine to Coca-Cola.

Sometimes Mami Wata is identified with powerful African deities such as Yemaya or Mawu-Lisu. She may be a creatrix, or a protector of nature and the wilds, even a prostitute.

"Mami Wata" is the common term for the manatees who live off the coast of West Africa, and they may have contributed to her image; in any case, the manatee is a symbol for her.

Mami Wata's worship continues today, assimilating local water spirits throughout Africa and the New World. Call upon her if your health issues involve fertility, sexuality, or body fluids of any kind; or if you feel a connection to the sea in its myriad, changing forms.

Mati Syra Zemlya: health, healing, fertility, sperm, childbirth, midwifery, protection from illness and epidemics

Mat Zemlya, Matka, Matka Ziemia, Mati, Mokosh, and more
Europe and Asia, Slavic: Russia

Mati Syra Zemlya, Moist Mother, or Mother Moist Earth, is Mother Earth, goddess of health, healing, midwifery, childbirth, protection from illness and epidemics, good fortune, justice, agriculture, community, divination and prophecy, and fertility—specifically the protector of sperm.

She is also goddess of justice, morality, promises and contracts, who witnesses oaths, and settles disputes. A promise, oath, or marriage vow was considered binding if the speaker swore in her name, placed one hand on the earth, swallowed a bit of dirt, or held some on his or her head as they made the promise.

In her aspect as Mokosh, she protects women, and rules home and hearth, traditional female occupations such as spinning and weaving, abundance, magick, and fate: she spins the web of life and death. She is sovereign over the *Domowije* (house spirits). The popular name for rain is "Mokosh's milk."

Mati Syra Zemlya was usually worshipped as the Earth itself, not in human likeness. However, she occasionally takes human form, as a black-skinned Slavic woman dressed in colorful, beribboned traditional garb, or as a primal figure with wild hair, long arms, and a big head. Statues of Mokosh show her sitting, hands raised, with horsemen to either side of her. For both, her symbols are soil, especially moist dark earth; stalks of wheat; hemp oil; and sheep.

Mati is wife to Svarog, a blacksmith god; or Yarilo, god of the springtime and plant growth; or Perun, the chief deity and sky god. Her son is Mikula, a hero-god and plowman.

Mati's festivals occur on Zemlya's Night (the 24th of every month), as well as May 1st, June 24th, and August 1st, when at dawn, hemp oil was ceremonially poured out to the four cardinal directions as farmers prayed for protection and good weather.

As Mokosh, her sacred day is Friday; and her feast day falls possibly on October 28th. Offerings to the goddess include vegetables, or strands of fleece left beside the stove at night.

As an Earth Mother goddess, as either Mati Syra Zemlya or Mokosh, she is akin to Ardvi Sura Anahita (Humid Mother of the Earth), an Iranian goddess; and also Semele or Gaia (Greek), Changing Woman (Native American), and Nerthus (German).

Mati is the most ancient deity of the Slavic world, and archaeologists have theorized that her worship began at least 30,000 years ago in the valley of the Don River, in Russia northeast of the Black Sea.

Mati Syra Zemlya, our Mother Earth, is the source of all life on this planet, and in a way, of all healing. As the supreme prophetess, she may assist with accurate diagnosis of health problems. To enlist her aid for any healing issue, particularly fertility or birthing, dig a small hole in the ground, pour in an offering of bread and wine, and speak to her of your needs. As you recover, give her thanks and stay in close touch with nature and the Earth, drawing upon her strength to restore your vitality.

Menrva: health, medicine, mental and emotional health

Menerva, Menrfa

Mediterranean, Etruscan

Menrva is a goddess of health, healing, and medicine, mental and emotional health, wisdom, wise counsel, prudence, schools, writing, the sciences, trade and commerce, war, art, crafts, poetry, spinning, weaving, smithcraft, strategy and war, and even weather, as a lightning goddess. She was called Goddess of a Thousand Works by Ovid, a reference to her many skills in different fields; like the Celtic Lugh, she seemed supremely competent at anything she set her hand to.

Her name may be a variant of Meneswā, She Who Measures, an ancient Italic moon goddess. However, it might have developed from a Proto-Indo-European root word *men-*, which relates to mind or memory.

Early depictions show her casting a lightning bolt, but later Etruscan artists borrowed Greek imagery of Athena, and showed her with a helmet, spear, and shield, and even wearing Athena's iconic breastplate with the Gorgon's head upon it. Appropriate symbols for Menrva might include lightning, the moon, the weapons and regalia of war, and probably owls.

Her original mythology is lost, and the stories about Menrva all seem to be lifted from the Greeks. She is depicted in art with prominent Greek figures such as ASCLEPIUS, Prometheus, Hermes, and Medusa, and appears to be a patron and protector of HERAKLES and Perseus.

The Roman goddess Minerva seems to be largely based on Menrva, with additions from Athena's lore. Menrva was part of a divine triad with her father Tinia (from whose head she was born) and her mother, the supreme Etruscan goddess Uni. The Romans, not very creative with theology, borrowed all three, honoring them as Jupiter, Minerva, and Juno.

Menrva's broad expertise should allow her to assist with any health or healing challenge; but given her ancient association with the mind, she may help particularly with mental health issues, including Alzheimer's; and her weather connection might help her understand emotional swings and mood changes as well.

The Birth of Menrva

Nehalennia: healing, fertility, emotional healing

Nehalaennia, Nehalenia

Europe, Celtic: Netherlands, Germany

Nehalennia is a goddess of healing, including emotional healing; seafaring, marine trade, shipping, and travel; and possibly fertility, plenty, horticulture, and the harvest. Most of her temples, altars, and votive inscriptions were clustered in the Netherlands on the coast, with some in Germany. She was invoked to grant safe passage across the North Sea, and certainly during storms at sea.

Her name may mean She Who is Near the Sea. *ne ("near") + *halen ("sea") + *ja ("she who is...").

Nehalennia appears in sculpture as a young woman wearing a short cloak. She is usually seated, with a friendly-looking dog at her feet. She holds a basket of apples and often loaves of special bread used for offerings at harvest time. A ship, ship's prow, or other marine symbols are sometimes beside her. Her symbols are dogs, ships, and overflowing baskets of loaves and apples.

The dog may be a guardian or protector; or related to her role as a healer; or might even be an allegorical symbol for fierce storms, called "the dogs of the sea" by one Roman author. The dog looks a bit like a greyhound or wolf-cross, but not very fierce.

Nehalennia's veneration began in the 2nd century BCE, if not earlier, and lasted at least until the 3rd century CE, when her main sanctuary was destroyed in a storm. More than a thousand years later, in 1645, a storm uncovered the ruins of one of her temples, and Nehalennia was rediscovered. Since then other temples have been found, and many altars and inscriptions. A close replica of one of her temples can be seen in Colijnsplaat.

Goddesses connected to her, or conflated, may include the Matres, a triple group of mother goddesses popular throughout Europe; the Norse goddess of apples Iðunn; the Germanic fertility goddess Nerthus; and the Vanir (Norse) couple Freyr and Freyja.

Nehalennia might best be invoked for health issues or injuries relating to the sea or water (such as emotional illness or distress), or for fertility. Considering that she has reemerged after being hidden so long, perhaps she would assist in clarity of diagnosis, revealing the underlying causes of an illness. Since she holds a basket of apples, she may be able to lead you to nutritional help for your health issue.

Section II, Part 1

Ninhursag: herbs, fertility, midwifery, newborns, motherhood

Aruru, Bau, Belet-Ili, Belitis Ninkarrak, Ga-Tum-Dug, Innini, Ki, Mami, Ninkharsag, Ninki, Ninlil, Ninmah, Ninmenna, Nintu

Mesopotamia, Sumerian

Ninhursag is a goddess of fertility, newborns, motherhood, healing, plants, herbal medicine, sovereignty, and the mountains. She is the patron of royalty, and the kings of Sumer were said to be nourished by her milk. It was she who placed the golden crown on each new king during the coronation ceremony in the temple. She is one of the seven greatest deities of the Sumerian pantheon.

She wears a tiered skirt and a horned headdress, with her hair styled in the shape of an omega, her major symbol, used as early as 3000 BCE. Sometimes she holds a leashed lion cub, and carries a staff or baton with the omega symbol at the top; sometimes she wears a wreath or crown of green leaves, and holds a leafy branch. The omega may represent a stylized womb, for it also appears in art depicting the Egyptian mother goddess Hathor.

The name Ninhursag means Lady of the Sacred Mountain. Her titles suggest how important she was to her culture: Great Queen, True and Great Lady of Heaven, Lady of Birth, Great Wife of Heaven, Faithful Wife, Womb

Goddess, Midwife of the Gods, Mother of All Children, and Mother of the Gods.

She is the wife and consort to Enki, Lord of the Earth god of water, intelligence, crafts, and creation; in one myth, Ninhursag helped Enki create humankind. In other myths, her husband is named Enlil or Ea.

In her primary myth, Ninhursag's great-granddaughter Uttu buried some of Enki's seed in the earth, and the first eight plants ever known grew there. Enki foolishly ate part of all of the plants without Ninhursag's permission, and became extremely ill. Ninhursag then ate the rest of all of the plants and bore eight new healing deities who personified the curative powers of the herbs, and they were able to restore Enki to health.

Her primary temple was called the Esaglia or the E-Kur, which means Temple on the Lofty Head or House of Mountain Deeps, in the city of Eridu. She had a second temple at Kish.

Call upon Ninhursag if herbal medicines are an important part of your healing strategy, or for problems with fertility or nursing a newborn. Call her by her divine titles, and use mountain imagery in your meditations.

Nodens: healing, childbirth, injuries sustained on the sea or while hunting, war wounds, emotional health, healer of dogs

Mars Nodens, Mars Nodontis, Mercury Nodens, Neptune Nodens, Noadatus, Nodons, Nuada, Nuadha, Núadu, Nudens

Europe, Romano-Celtic: Britain, possibly Gaul

Nodens is a god associated with healing, emotional health, childbirth, the sea, hunting, dogs, and healing of dogs.

His name may come from the Celtic root *noudont-* or *noudent-*, which can mean to acquire, have the use of, use, catch, fish, or entrap; but some say it might mean "cloud-maker" or "wealth-bringer."

Images of Nodens seem to be rare, though it seems that Romans visualized him as a sea god similar to Neptune, sometimes riding a chariot pulled by sea creatures. His symbols, or at least associated images, include sea gods, tritons, fish, dolphins, sea monsters, and dogs. (Note the dog dancing on his nose on the coin!)

One wonders, however, about the nine dog statues found in Nodens' temple complex at Lydney Park in England. They look somewhat like Irish wolfhounds. Are these simply the standard companions to healers all over Europe and the Mediterranean (one theory is that dogs were thought to be natural healers, because they licked their own wounds, cleansing and healing them); or is it possible that Nodens sometimes shape-shifted into canine form?

The central area of his Lydney Park temple has the remnants of a mosaic floor with marine designs: fish, dolphins, and sea monsters. There are dormitory rooms where sick supplicants might sleep, seeking guidance or visions of the god in their dreams. Many artifacts, probably offerings, have been discovered on the grounds, including hundreds of bracelets and pins, and thousands of coins.

Nodens is conflated with such Roman gods as Neptune, Mars, and Mercury, as well as the hunting god Silvanus; and seems linked to the Welsh Nudd or Llud Llaw Ereint, and Nuada of the Silver Hand, first king of the fabled Tuatha Dé Danann in Ireland. Nodens is also similar to Njord, Norse Vanir god of seamanship, sailing, and wind, who can ignite storms or calm the waves.

You might seek Nodens as an ally if you have injuries related to sailing or the sea, or hunting; or war wounds; or if you desire a safe and quick birthing for your baby. He may help you calm emotional storms or distress; or intervene if your dog is hurt or ill.

Statue of a dog, found at the Lydney Park temple

Pajau Yan: health, healing, menstruation, immortality, peaceful death, resurrection

Paja Yan, Pajan Yan, Pajau Tan
Southeast Asia: Vietnam, Chams

Pajau Yan is a kind and good goddess of health, healing, beauty, good fortune, time, immortality, night, the moon, and menstruation. She is especially attentive to the needs of women who call upon her.

She is often called Lady Moon, and lives on that shining satellite. She sees the spirits of the departed as they pass into the next life, and gives each one ease in their passage, and hope for the future, with a gift of flowers: the "Flowers of Transition."

Symbols appropriate to her shrines and rituals include moon images and flowers.

Pajau Yan began her life on Earth, but became so adept at healing—even raising people from the dead—that the gods sent her to live on the moon, lest she completely upset the natural cycle of life and death. There she engineers lunar eclipses, as a way to give honor to the sun.

She is a beloved goddess who is invited to all sacrificial rituals, but her special day is the first day after the full moon, as it begins to wane. Then she is given offerings of fruit.

Pajau Yan can be a loving ally in your quest for restored health, and perhaps especially for gynecological maladies, including difficulties pertaining to menstruation.

If your medical situation seems desperate, ask her to give you peace and healing; and if necessary, she will give you flowers and keep you company on the next stage of your journey.

Sekhmet: healing, medicine, surgery, bone-setting, sunburn, sunstroke

Sakhmet, Sakhmis, Sekhet, and more
Africa, Egyptian

Sekhmet is a goddess of healing, medicine, surgery, bone-setting, justice, war, courage, strength, physical prowess, wild animals, the sun, sunburn, and sunstroke. She protected the royal dynasty, and led the pharaohs into battle. As a solar goddess, she personified the fierce, dangerous heat of the sun in the hottest part of the day. The deserts of Egypt were created by her fiery breath.

Sekhmet's name means The Powerful One, and she was called The Great One of Healing, but also Goddess of Fire and Heat, Lady of Slaughter, Mistress of Dread, She Who Mauls, and The One Before Whom Evil Trembles.

Hundreds of statues of Sekhmet survive, nearly always showing her as a powerful, lioness-headed woman standing or sitting stiffly erect, either naked or dressed in blood-red garments, wearing a solar disk and the *uraeus* (cobra form) on her head, and holding an *ankh* or *sistrum*. Occasionally she was depicted simply as a fierce lioness. Her symbols, of course, were the lioness, the solar disk, and uraeus.

Her father is Ra, the sun god. Her sister or alter ego is Bast, cat-headed goddess of joy, dance, music, love, protection, family, and the gentle, life-giving power of the sun.

In her major myth, Sekhmet almost destroyed mankind when Ra sent her to punish mortals who had conspired against him. Sekhmet's rage and violence threatened to exterminate all humans, alarming the gods. Thinking quickly, the gods dyed great vats of beer red, and poured them out in her path. Believing it to be blood, she drank it all and became too intoxicated to continue.

She could be a wrathful and dangerous goddess, despite her healing skills. To appease her, priestesses of Sekhmet performed a daily ritual, each day before a different statue of her. At the beginning of each new year, her festival drew tens of thousands of celebrants to her temples. Here, priestesses and commoners alike drank enormous quantities of beer and wine, and danced until they dropped to the music of *sistrums*, lutes, and drums played day and night, in a ritual reenactment of the drunken end of her terrifying rampage. Special ceremonies were also performed following any battle, to encourage an end to bloodshed.

Sekhmet had a great temple at Taremu in the delta region of the Nile, later called Leontopolis by the Greeks. The grounds included an enclosure for tame lions. In a temple at Luxor connected to Sekhmet, the famous pharaoh Queen Hatshepsut had a "porch of drunkenness" built to commemorate the divine lioness.

Sekhmet's is closely connected with Bast, and associated with Hathor, the cow goddess of motherhood, joy, music and dance; the cobra goddess and patron of pharaohs, Wadjet; Ma'at, goddess of truth, order, and justice; and the rain goddess Tefnut.

Call upon Sekhmet when great skill is needed in surgery; when broken bones must be set; and for sunburn or sunstroke. Call her sister/counterpart Bast for balance, or when alcohol abuse, violent behavior, or injury from violence are present.

Shaushka: sexuality, androgyny, bisexuality, health, healing

Šauša, Šauška, Šawuška, Shaushga

Mesopotamia/Anatolia, Hurrian and Hittite

Shaushka is a goddess of fertility, love, sexuality, relationships, war, and healing. She seems to be bisexual and perhaps androgynous; sometimes she is shown in reliefs with gods, and sometimes with goddesses. She is patron of love and harmony in marriage, but also the risky, even dangerous aspects of love.

Sculptures and reliefs of Shaushka show her as a winged human astride a lion (or with one beside her), dressed in clothing that is neither feminine nor completely masculine, and carrying a gold chalice, or often an axe and other weapons. Though her medical skills are powerful, she looks more the warrior than healer. Her symbol is the lion.

Shaushka is closely associated with Ishtar, the great goddess of Mesopotamia, and was sometimes even called Ishtar.

Her importance as a goddess of healing is suggested in a missive included in the Amarna Letters (1350-1335 BCE) to the Pharaoh. The friendly letter is from the king of Mitanni, and apparently it accompanied the loan of a statue of Shaushka to the ailing Egyptian king. It suggests that this healing goddess has traveled between the nations before, and reads in part:

> ... just as earlier she dwelt there and they honored her, may my brother now honor her 10 times more than before.... then) at (his) pleasure let her go so that she may come back. May Šauška, the mistress of heaven, protect us, my brother and me, 100,000 years, and may our mistress grant both of us great joy....

You may wish to invoke Shaushka if you are bisexual and/or androgynous, as she is a kindred spirit; if your health challenges are putting stress on your marriage, and you want to preserve or restore harmony with your partner; or if you simply need a fierce, protective, and commanding goddess by your side as you face and conquer your illness.

Sirona: healing of illness and injury, healing springs

Thirona, Tsirona

Europe, Celtic: Gaul, Germany

Sirona is a goddess of healing, healing springs and waters, rulership, fertility, and abundance.

Her name is from a proto-Celtic root word meaning "star," and means "stellar" or "astral."

A typical statue or bas-relief shows Sirona dressed in a long gown (sometimes nude to the waist), and wearing a star-studded diadem with attached veil. She usually has a serpent wrapped around her lower arm, drinking from a bowl in her hand. In her other hand she holds a scepter, a bowl of eggs, a cornucopia, or fruits and grain. All of these, and stars, are her symbols.

Her temples were often built at hot springs or holy wells. One temple complex at a remote site in Germany was created around a spring, which supplied an indoor therapeutic pool. Several statues of Sirona and APOLLO offered a silent benediction to the supplicants who came here.

We see a strong Greco-Roman influence on the cult of Sirona, since she is often paired with Apollo, usually as Apollo GRANNUS or Apollo BORVO. Sometimes she appears with HERAKLES, MENRVA, or ASCLEPIUS.

Sirona can help heal all injury and illness, enhance fertility, inspire you to take charge of your own health, and bring abundant resources to your quest for healing. She works well with Apollo; consider creating a shrine to both and invoking them together.

Sitala: cholera, dysentery, all infectious diseases, cools fevers, emotional health

Jyestha, Shakti, Sheetala, Shitala

Asia: India, Nepal, Bangladesh, Pakistan

Sitala, with several of her sisters, cures cholera, dysentery, measles, smallpox, and other infectious diseases, cures skin diseases, cools and soothes those with fevers, drives away demons, ghouls, and despairing thoughts, and brings emotional health.

Sitala means Coolness, or One Who Cools. She is called Ma or Mata, which both mean simply Mother, as well as Jagrani (Queen of the World), Karunamayi (She Who Is Full of Mercy), Mangala (The Auspicious One), and Dayamayi (She Who Is Full of Grace and Kindness).

She is shown as a young maiden, sometimes riding a donkey. In her (sometimes) four hands she carries a winnowing-fan, a short broom, a pot of pulses, a jar of cool water, a drinking cup, or sometimes medicinal herbs. All of these are her symbols, as well as neem leaves, an herbal remedy for skin diseases. With the broom she can either spread disease or brush it off people; as with many healing deities, she has complete power over illness, either to cause or to cure it.

Sitala is an incarnation of the great warrior goddess Durga, who in turn is an aspect of fierce Kali. Some see her as a form of

Parvati, mighty Shiva's consort. Among the ancient Dravidian peoples in the south of India, her equivalent is Mariamman. She is personified as the spring season under the name Vasant.

According to one myth, the warrior goddess Durga chose to incarnate as a little girl named Katyayani, as part of a plan to destroy all the demons who preyed upon the human world. When the fever demon, Jwarasur, began to make her young friends sick, Katyayani healed them, then manifested as Sitala Devi to carry the battle to the rest of the world, destroying disease and purifying the blood of children everywhere.

Katyayani had asked her friend Batuk to face the fever demon, but Jwarasur killed the young hero, but Batuk magically reanimated as the terrible warrior Bhairev, who was actually the god Shiva. His appearance alone should have frightened the demon to death: the warrior was a towering black figure, clad in a massive tiger skin and rattling skulls, glaring with three fiery eyes, and wielding weapons in his several arms. In a fierce battle, Bhairev skewered the demon with his mighty trident and proved to be a formidable ally to Sitala, herself a formidable goddess.

Sitala is popular all over India and neighboring nations, among Hindus and Buddhists, and in communities that mix these faiths with indigenous spiritual traditions.

Call upon Sitala and her ally Bhairev to heal any illness, especially those involving fever, and to banish negative energies, from demons to despairing thoughts. Honor them with many candles and sacred songs or chants, and know that your companions are fierce and powerful warriors against disease, who will stand with you until you have regained health and vitality.

Section II, Part 1

Tawaret: fertility, pregnancy, childbirth, newborns, nursing mothers, children, death and rebirth

Apet, Opet, Rertrertu, Taouris, Taueret, Ta-Urt, Taurt, Ta-weret, Taweret, Thouéris, Toeris, Tuart, Tuat, and others

Africa, Egyptian

Tawaret is a hippopotamus goddess of fertility, childbirth, nursing mothers, protection of newborns and children, child-rearing, regeneration, protection of the home, protection against evil, the fertility and rejuvenation of the annual flooding of the River Nile, death and rebirth (including the daily rebirth of the sun), and guidance through the underworld. Female hippopotami were revered because they vigorously protect their young.

Her name means She Who is Great, or simply Great One. She is called Mistress of the Horizon, Lady of Heaven, Mistress of Pure Water, and Mistress of the Birth House. Originally a sky goddess, her constellation is Ursa Major.

She is shown as a bipedal, breasted, often very pregnant hippopotamus with a crocodile's back, or a crocodile tail, or sometimes the crocodile is on her back, or upright in her right hand. The *Sa* hieroglyph, meaning "protection" (representing the goddess' uterine blood, which could bestow eternal life) is under her left hand. Sometimes her hands are the paws of a lioness.

In myth, she helps Horus, the divine son of Isis and Osiris, to vanquish the evil god Set. In a late myth, Tawaret and Bes were the sow and the dwarf who actually raise Horus.

Religious devotion of Tawaret began in the Middle Kingdom. So central was her role in the lives of all Egyptians that her veneration continued even when Akhenaten forbade polytheism in favor of the worship of Aten. Tawaret developed a significant cult outside of Egypt as well, in the Levant, Crete, Greece, and Nubia.

All kinds of sacred and ritual objects bearing her likeness were popular in Egypt, until the conversion to Islam. She appeared on amulets worn by mothers and their children, on household furniture, and especially on ivory (or hippopotamus bone) wands used by nurses and midwives to draw symbols of protection in the sand (possibly the *Sa* hieroglyph) around the childbirth bed, and in rituals to protect infants. During the New Kingdom, a popular product was a pitcher shaped like Tawaret, often with pouring holes in her nipples. Any liquid dispensed from it was considered to be ritually purified.

She is conflated with other Egyptian hippopotamus goddesses, including Ipet, The Nurse, who is a deity of birth, child rearing, and general caretaking, and Reret, The Sow. When powerful Egyptian goddesses like ISIS, Mut, and Hathor assumed a protective role, they assumed the form of Tawaret, and Tawaret absorbed their qualities, even to wearing the solar disk. She also appears as Neith, protective mother to Sobek, the crocodile god.

Wear a hippopotamus talisman and call upon Tawaret if you are pregnant, or a mother who needs protection and healing, or if your children do; or if you choose to become the protective force in your home. Charge pure water with her fierce maternal power and drink it, to fill your heart with strength and courage and stand as the guardian of your home and family.

Section II, Part 1

Uretsete and Naotste: health, healing, teacher

I'tc'ts'ity and Nau'tsity, Liatiku and Nautsity, Utctsityi and Nausity, Utset and Nowutset,

North America, Southwest: Cochiti and other Pueblo Nations

These are divine sisters inextricably linked in the stories of Pueblo peoples. Uretsete is a mother goddess of health, healing, knowledge, family and community, and teacher of medicine men.

In most pueblos Uretsete is the mother of the Pueblo nations; and Naotste is the mother of alien peoples, including the Navajos and the white settlers. They were both sung into being by Sussistanako, or Spider Woman. Uretsete means Bringer to Life, and Naotste can be translated as More of Everything in the Basket.

When they emerged from the underworld into the light, they were charged with traveling the earth with seeds and animals to spread life all over, but tension built between them. Uretsete, short and plain, was good-hearted; whereas the taller, imposing Naotste was unfriendly and quarrelsome. Their rivalry culminated in a contest where they had to identify the tracks of wild creatures, and the correctly named creature then belonged to the sister who named it. Uretsete won, and Naotste's penalty was death.

After Uretsete's People had migrated to the south, perhaps from the Chaco Canyon area, they fell upon hard times and many grew sick. First Coyote, then two men were sent as messengers to ask her for help. She trained the two men to become medicine men, and they spread the arts of healing among the People.

Only call upon Uretsete for help if you are from the Pueblos, or guided by a Pueblo elder. Her living tradition deserves respect, and an outsider could easily invoke her incorrectly.

Vejovis: protection from plagues and natural disasters

Vejove

Mediterranean, Roman

Vejovis is a god of healing and protection from plagues, disease, and natural disasters such as earthquakes and volcanoes. Some have called him the patron of the persecuted: slaves, immigrants, and those who refuse to give up the fight for a desperate cause. His temples were sanctuaries for those who fled oppression and injustice. If called to aid a just cause, he could deceive and confuse its enemies.

Vejovis is thought to be extremely ancient, one of the first gods to exist. His name can be translated as Not-Jove, implying a divine antithesis to the sky-father god—perhaps he is a pre-Roman underworld deity, since legends hint that he could help lost souls escape from the nether regions.

In art he appears as a young, beardless man, variously holding lightning bolts, a bunch of arrows, a Roman spear, or a laurel wreath. A goat stands beside him. These are his symbols.

His center of worship was in Rome, where he had temples on the Capitoline Hill and Tiber Island. Three major festivals honored Vejovis: one sometime in January, plus March 7th and May 21st. Goats were sacrificed to him in March, to protect the people from plagues.

Though similar to the Greek god ASCLEPIUS, he is sometimes identified with the sun god APOLLO, or the infant Jupiter.

Ask for his protection and healing when contagious diseases, epidemics, or natural disasters threaten us.

Part 2
Additional Goddesses and Gods

How can you work with a deity if very little is known about them? Surprisingly, it may be easy. Book knowledge and scholarly research is never complete, and often scholars contradict each other anyway. The solution? Go directly to the source.

Many of the following deities are just a strong in their healing capabilities as those featured in the previous part, but less is known about some of them. Sometimes all we could find in our research was that they are "a healing god (or goddess)." Period. Others are actually well-known for their other attributes, but not so much for healing.

If a deity intrigues you, try to get better acquainted through meditation, dream work, or divination. Use the tools of spirit to learn more about a spirit being. Often a name or an image, if it's all you have, can unlock deep knowledge.

If a god or goddess is known chiefly as a sun god, or perhaps an earth goddess, this does not mean you should discount their healing powers. Power in one field may well translate into strength in another. So use this list as a starting point for exploring deities less familiar to you. They can become some of your strongest allies.

NAME	CULTURE	DESCRIPTION
Agathos Diamon, Agathadeamon, Agthodiamon	Mediterranean, Greek	Deity of good fortune, health, and life.
Ah Uaynih	Central America, Guatemala, Chorti	Goddess of health, healing; and restful sleep for males.
Ahau-Chamahez	Central America, Maya	Lord of the Magic Tooth, god of medicine.
Aherah	Mesopotamia, Phoenicia	Goddess of birth, blessings, health, divination, law, luck, carpentry, masonry, and wisdom. The Mother of All Wisdom, Proprietress of Universal Law. Symbols: brick and a wooden pole.
Ahnt Kai'	Central America, Mexico, Seri	Goddess of health, healing, education, knowledge, arts, ceremonies; mother and guardian.
Ahurani	Middle East, Persia	Goddess of fertility, growth, harvest, health, insight, longevity, luck, and prosperity. Symbols: water and beverages.
Aialila'axa	North America, Northwest, Bella Coola	Goddess of the moon and night, and healing, who protects from illness and death.
Aibheaog, Aibheaeg	Europe, Celtic, Ireland	Fire goddess whose sacred well held waters that could cure toothache, if the supplicant left a white stone.
Ai tūpua'i	Pacific, Polynesia, Tahiti, Society Islands (Ta'aroa)	Goddess of war, health, and healing.
Aja	Africa, Yoruba; Caribbean, Santeria	Orisha of the forest and wild animals. She is also patron of herbal healers, and a teacher to all who practice the healing arts.
Ajysit	Europe and Asia, Slavic, Siberia, Yakut	Goddess of birth, fate, nursing, ceremonies, heaven and hell. Called The Milk Lake Mother.

Additional Gods and Goddesses

NAME	CULTURE	DESCRIPTION
Akerbeltz	Europe, Basque	Goddess of healing, health, protection from disease, beauty, charity, peace, harvest, and thankfulness. Symbols: rainbows and healing amulets.
'Alahtin	North America, California, Chumash	Moon goddess of cleansing and purification, health, healing, prosperity, the calendar, the tides, and menstrual periods.
Alauna	Europe, Celtic	A river goddess associated with healing; see Alaunus.
Alaunus	Europe, Celtic	God of healing prophecy, and the sun; see Alauna.
Almoshi	Europe and Asia, Slavic, Siberia, Trans-Baikal Buriat	Goddess of health and healing, especially domesticated animals, particularly cattle.
Amenhetep	Africa, Egyptian	God of healing.
Ameretat, Amardad, Amererat, Murdad	Persia	God of all green plants, health, long life.
Angak	North America, Hopi	A kachina spirit of healing and rain, shown with long, black hair, holding an evergreen branch and with raincloud symbols on his costume.
Anna Parenna	Mediterranean, Roman	Goddess of cycles, grounding, kindness, longevity, and peace. Name means Enduring Year. Symbols: wine and circles (wheels, rings, wreaths).
Anubis, Anpu, Sekhem Em Pet	Africa, Egyptian	Jackal-headed god of funeral rites and the underworld, protector and judge of the dead, anesthetics, hospital stays, medicine, surgery, justice, truth, wisdom, and much more.
Apolonia, Saint	South America, Brazil, Ita	Goddess or saint of healing, especially for toothache or other dental problems.

NAME	CULTURE	DESCRIPTION
Ashvins, Ashwini, Dasra and Nasatya	India, Hindu	Divine twins, physicians of the gods and patrons of Ayurvedic medicine. Shown as twin horsemen, or both in a golden chariot, sometimes as men with horses' heads.
Atepomarus, Apollo Atepomarus	Europe, Mediterranean, Gauls, Romans	Healing god sometimes called Apollo Atepomarus. His name means Great Horseman, or Owner of a Great Horse.
Aveta	Europe, Celtic	Water goddess who had a healing spring at Trier in Germany, and was shown as a nursing mother.
Badger Old Woman	North America, Southwest, Pueblo	Goddess of childbirth, hunting, wild animals, ceremonies, and the gateway to the other world of the kachinas.
Bai Suzhen, Bai Zu Shen	Asia, China	Known as Madame White Snake, White Lady, or the White Maiden. An immortal who can present as a lovely maiden or transform into a huge and powerful snake. In her form as a human woman, she falls in love with a mortal man. Together they open an herbal medicine shop, and become renowned as great healers.
Bast, Bastet, Pasht	Africa, Egyptian	Cat-headed goddess of the gentle sunlight, the moon, fertility, childbirth, protection against disease, healing, joy, dance, music, and more.
Bebhionn	Europe, Celtic, Ireland	Giant supernatural woman from the Isle of Women off the Irish west coast. She commanded all powers of healing, and traveled with magickal birds.
Bel, Belenus, Belinos, Beli Mawr	Europe, Celtic	Great god of sun, fire, purification, fertility, healing, prosperity, cattle, and more. Name means Shining.

Additional Gods and Goddesses

NAME	CULTURE	DESCRIPTION
Bhaishajyaguru, Bhaisajyaguru, Man-La, Sang-Gyeman-Gyila-Bduryr-O-Chi-Gyal-Po (Tibet), Yao-Shih Fu (China)	India/Buddhist the master session	God of healing and sex change, master physician, God of healing and spells. Shown as blue. Rules the east, and holds fruit in his right hand.
Big Black Meteor Star	North America, Plains, Pawnee	Goddess of stars, planets, healing, and knowledge. Called Star of Magic; teaches medicine people their craft.
Binzuru, Binzuku	Asia, Japan, Buddhist	Originally mortal, deified because of miraculous abilities to heal the sick.
Buschgrossmutter	Europe, German	The queen of the Buschfrauen, elves with mossy feet, who lived in hollow trees in virgin forests, and knew all the secrets of herbs and healing. Name means The Grandmother of the Bushes.
Caolainn	Europe, Celtic, Ireland	Goddess who ruled a healing well, and could cure any ailment of the eyes. Is a form of the Cailleach.
Carmentis, Carmenta, Nicostrata, Postverta	Mediterranean, Roman	Goddess of birth, children, fertility, healing, prophecy. Name means a spell or charm in the form of a song. Symbols: music and babies.
Ceacht	Europe, Celtic, Ireland	Goddess of medicine. Name means Lesson.
Chin Mu	Asia, China	Goddess of health and long life, femininity, and magick; an ageless, beautiful woman. Name means Golden Mother. Symbols: peach, mulberry, cats, and golden things.
Cit-Bolon-Tum	Maya	God of medicine, called Boar of the Nine Tusks. His treatments involve nine precious stones.
Cocamama	South America, Peru	Goddess of healing, health, happiness, love, sexuality, the Earth, nature, selfishness, life and death. Mother of the coca plant.

173

NAME	CULTURE	DESCRIPTION
Corn Mother, Mother Sunset Yellow	North America, Plains, Arikara, Pawnee, Cheyenne, Mandan, Hidatsa	The maize plant personified as a goddess of health, healing, agriculture, fertility, knowledge, ceremonies, and medicine bundles.
Coventina	Europe, England	River goddess of a sacred well in Northumberland, and goddess of healing, inspiration, and prophecy.
Cura	Mediterranean, Roman	The Goddess who created humans from clay, and provides cures for all diseases.
Cybele	Mediterranean, Roman	Goddess of health, strength, love, relationships, victory, and humor. Symbols: meteorite or black stone, pine tree, and key.
Damara	Europe, England	Goddess of fertility, well-being, health, kindness, abundance, and luck. Associated with the month of May. Symbols: flowers and greenery.
Damia	Mediterranean, Greek	Goddess of health, especially women's health; worshipped only by women
Damona	Europe, Gaul	Goddess who protects pets and domestic animals, and preserves their health.
Derzelas, Darzalas	Mediterranean, Dacian or Thracian	God of health and the vitality of the human spirit, as well as abundance and the underworld. Shown holding cornucopias. Sacred games were held every five years to honor him.
Dhatri	India, Hindu	Solar deity and god of health and domestic tranquility. Name means Earth. Can be invoked by drawing sacred diagrams and chanting certain hymns.
Dinawagan	Southeast Asia, Philippines, Apayao	Goddess of health and healing.

Additional Gods and Goddesses

NAME	CULTURE	DESCRIPTION
Dziwozony, Divozenky, Divi-Te-Zeni	Europe, Slavic	The Wild Women of the Woods, who lived in burrows, and knew the secrets of herbal medicine. Shown as red and square-headed, with long fingers.
Eeyeekalduk	North America, Inuit	God of healing medicine and good health. Shown as a small man with a black face, lives in a small stone. He drew illness from the patient into himself, through his eyes, and could also send illness from himself to others through his eyes.
Epona	Europe, Celtic	Goddess of horses, fertility, maternity, healing springs, sovereignty, prosperity, dogs, and more. Name means The Great Mare.
Famien	Africa, Guinea	God of fertility and good health. Carried one or two knives in a medicine bag.
Febris	Mediterranean, Roman	Goddess who could cause or cure malaria and fevers. Said be be an honest and shrewd deity.
Fons	Mediterranean, Roman	Goddess of fountains, springs, fresh drinking water, healing, and thankfulness. The cleansing and healing power of clean water.
Fukurokujin	Asia, Japan, Buddhist	One of the seven deities of luck, the god of health and longevity. Shown with a stork, a cane, and a Book of Fate.
Ganga	India, Hindu	Goddess of the river Ganges, and purifications, cleansing, health, wellness, and mercy. Stands on a sea monster. Symbols: water and yellow things.
Gefn	Europe, Norse and Teutonic	Joyous goddess of the sun, spring, health, fertility, love, abundance, divination, and growth. Name means Giver. Symbols: all green and growing things.

NAME	CULTURE	DESCRIPTION
Glanis (Celtic), Valetudo (Roman)	Europe/ Mediterranean, Gaul, Rome	God associated with a healing spring where pilgrims bathed, in southern France.
Glispa	North America, Navajo	Goddess of magick, ceremonies, health, healing, knowledge, sand painting, and feather offerings. Brought the healing chant, Hozoni, to the people. May have been a form of the goddess Estsanatlehi, or Turquoise Woman.
Guabonito	Caribbean, Haiti, Taino	Sea goddess of medicines, health, healing, and ceremonies.
Gulliveig	Scandanavia, Vanir	Goddess of magick, healing, and prophesy. Name means Golden Branch.
Gunnloed	Europe, Teutonic	Goddess of health, fertility, protection, wisdom, poetry, and creativity. Giantess who holds a cup of mead. Symbols: apples, and cauldron or cup
Habetrot	Europe, England	Goddess of spinning, healing, and magickal protective garments.
Habondia, Habonde	Europe, Celtic	Witchy goddess of abundance, fertility, cleansing, health, joy, luck, and magick. Dance around her ritual fire and let its smoke cleanse you. Symbols: ale and fires.
Hadui	North America, Iroquois	God of disease, medicine, and cures, seen as a hunchbacked dwarf.
Ha'iaka	Polynesian	Goddess of healing, flowers, and magick. Born in the shape of an egg.
Haltia, Holdja	Europe, Finno-Ugric, Baltic Finn	Goddess of the home, health, healing, the directions, luck, and domesticated animals.
Haoma	Middle East, Persia, Zoroastrian	God of health, healing, and fertility named for a divine plant, the King of Herbs, thought to be ephedra. Associated with purification and

Additional Gods and Goddesses

NAME	CULTURE	DESCRIPTION
		the continuity of life—even including immortality; and is patron of the priesthood.
Haurvatat, Ameretat, Khurdad, Amardad	Middle East, Persia, Zoroastrian	Goddesses of health and immortality, water, vegetation, and wealth.
Heqet, Heket, Hekt, Heqt, and more	Africa, Egyptian	Goddess of primordial waters, fertility, childbirth, and regeneration. Giver of life. Shown as a frog.
Hertha	Europe, Teutonic	Goddess of fertility, health, longevity, rebirth, tradition, nature, and domesticated animals. She descends through the smoke of a fire and brings gifts. Symbols: dormant trees and snow.
Hesy-Ra	Africa, Egyptian	An official and priest of Egypt, during the reign of Pharoah (and physician) Djoser. The first person in the history of that ancient land to be recognized as a professional dentist. Deified after death.
Hexe	Europe, Germanic	Goddess of health, healing herbs, magick charms, banishing curses, and teaching spells and charms. A favorite of German Witches.
Hi'iaka I ka pua'ena'ena, Hiata ta bu enaena	Pacific, Polynesia, Hawaii	Goddess of healing, leis, and kava—the drink of the gods; travel and trade. As a healer, she is named Kuku 'ena I kea hi ho'omau honua. She is Pele's sister.
Hina lau limu kala	Pacific, Polynesia, Hawaii	Sea goddess of health, healing, medicines from the sea, and ceremonies.
Hina tahu tahu	Pacific, Polynesia, Tahiti	Goddess of healing, divination, and fate.
Hina uri	Pacific, Polynesia, Hawaii, New Zealand, Maori	Goddess of the night, dark moon, and childbirth. She is Māui's sister.

177

NAME	CULTURE	DESCRIPTION
Hooded Spirits, Genii Cucullati	Europe and Mediterranean, Celtic and Roman especially in the Rhineland.	Spirits associated with health and fertility, and who sometimes carry egg-shapes and swords, perhaps symbolizing life, death, and rebirth.
Huchi	Asia, Japan	Goddess of fire, cleansing, health, protection from disease, energy, light, and the harvest. Her fires cleanse, energize, and protect.
Ianuaria	Europe, Celtic	Goddess revered at a sacred spring and shrine in Burgundy. Shown as a young girl with curly hair, holding pan-pipes, and wearing a pleated coat. May be a healing goddess, or a music goddess, or both, since music can help heal.
Ibabasag	Southeast Asia, Philippines, Bukidnon	Goddess of pregnancy and childbirth.
Imaymana Viracocha	South America, Inca	God who tells mortals of the healing properties of plants, and warns of dangerous ones.
Imhotep, I-Em-Hetep, Iemhetep, Imhetep, Imuthes (Greek)	Africa, Egyptian	An Egyptian polymath, skilled in medicine, engineering, architecture, philosophy and more. Lived in the 27th century BCE, he was a priest of Ra. Deified 2,000 years after his death. God of medicine, healing, physicians, herbs, drugs, sleep to heal suffering and pain, learning, and more. Name means The One Who Comes in Peace.
Iovantucarus	Europe/ Mediterannean, Gaul, Rome	God of healing who protected youth. Associated with Lenus Mars and also Mercury. Liked pet birds as offerings.
Itchita	Siberia, Yukut	Birch tree goddess of healing and protection; the spirits of grass and trees are her tiny helpers.

Additional Gods and Goddesses

NAME	CULTURE	DESCRIPTION
Itzamna, Itzmatul, Izamna and many more	Central America, Mayan	God of healing, the sky, creation, writing, and fertile fields. Can bring the dead back to life. Shown with a red hand.
Ix U Sihnal	Central America, Mexican, Yucatec Maya	Moon goddess of health, healing, procreation, childbirth, water, and the curing of ulcers.
Ixazalvoh, Ixzaluoh	Central America, Mayan	Goddess of healing, childbirth, sexuality, weaving, and prophecy.
Ixtab	Central America, Mexican, Yucatec Maya	Goddess of medicine, health, healing, justice, water, the moon, homes, weaving, rainbow, heaven and hell, and those who die in childbirth, battle, or by suicide.
Ixtlilton	Central America, Aztec	God of healing and medicine, called The Little Black One. Thought to reside in an obsidian mask that has the power to bring peaceful sleep to children. His brother is the god of well-being or good luck.
Izu No Me Mo Kami	Asia, Japan	Goddess of purification, cleansing, health, mediation, and rites of purification with water or fire.
Janguli	India, Bengali	Golden snake goddess with six hands, who can heal snakebite.
Jun Ti	Asia, China, Buddhism	Goddess of fertility, long life, wisdom, luck, power, and protection. Lives on Polaris. Symbols: dragons, the sun, the moon, and the numbers three and eighteen.
Juturna	Mediterranean, Roman	Goddess of healing springs; bathing in her fountain healed and renewed health.
Kamrusepas, Kamrusepa	Middle East, Hittite	Goddess of healing, medicine, magick, chanting, ritual purification, and spells. Removes or redirect the anger of gods and men, so that it is harmless.

179

NAME	CULTURE	DESCRIPTION
Kāne kua'ana	Pacific, Polynesia, Hawaii	Human woman who transformed into a dragon or lizard goddess of health, healing, fishing, abundance, reptiles, and creatures of the sea. Honor her with a fire altar, and she will protect you from sickness and bring you wealth.
Kapo	Pacific, Polynesia, Hawaii	Goddess of childbirth, and termination of pregnancy.
Katsin Numka Majan	Southeast Asia, Burma, Katchins	Goddess of healing, especially the lungs, heart, liver, and other internal organs. Called the Mother of Vital Organs.
Kattakju	North America, Arctic, Baffin Land Inuit	Goddess of healing, who helps shamans in their work with those who are ill.
Khensu, Khonsu, Aa, Khons	Africa, Egyptian	God of healing, regeneration, and the moon. His name means Traveler.
Khors	Europe, Slavic	God of health and hunting. Appears as a stallion.
Kinich Ahau, Kinish-Kakimo	Central America, Maya	God of healing, medicine, and the sun. His name means The Lord of the Face of the Sun.
Kiri Amma	Indian Ocean, Sri Lanka	Seven-fold goddess who heals diseases in children, and blesses nursing mothers. Name can mean Grandmother, Milk Mother, or Wet Nurse.
Komwidapokuwia	North America, Southwest, Yavapai	Creator goddess of life, magick, healing, and protection for healers.
Lada	Europe, Swiss	Goddess who sweeps away illness with her skirts, and ushers in the spring. Goddess of protection, kinship, energy, and joy. Symbols: birch tree and bells.

Additional Gods and Goddesses

NAME	CULTURE	DESCRIPTION
Lenus, Lenus Mars, Ocelus Vellaunus	Europe/ Mediterannean, Gaul, Rome, Greece	Healing and protective god is depicted as a warrior with a Corinthian-style helmet. His sanctuaries included temples, shrines, baths, sleeping rooms for pilgrims, and even theaters. Worked with the goddesses Ancamna Victoria and Inciona.
L'etsa'aplelana	North America, Northwest Bella Coola	Goddess of magick, ceremonies, healing, and the initiation of medicine people.
Loco, Loko	Caribbean, Vodun	The loa of healers and plants, particularly trees. A Rada (benevolent) Loa. He and his wife **Ayizan** are believed to be the first priest (houngan) and priestess (mambo), guardians of initiation and the correct rites.
Maddarakka	Europe, Scandinavia, Finno Ugric, Sami	Goddess of healing, caring for the spirits of the unborn, and childbirth. Called Old Woman.
Mahalbiya	Africa, Housa	Goddess who causes skin diseases and ulcers, yet gives the power to heal them to dancers whom she possesses during ritual.
Mamaldi	Europe/Asia, Slavic, Siberia, Amur	Creator goddess of health, healing, and magick.
Maponus, Maponos, Apollo Maponus, Mabon	Europe, Britain, Gaul, also Rome	God of healing and springs, poetry, song, and youthful beauty. Name means Young Boy, and Son, or Great Son.
Māri, Mariamman, Maariamma, Mariaai, Amman, Aatha	India, Hindu	South Indian mother goddess, and deity of disease and rain. Associated with the goddesses Parvati, Durga, and Shitaladevi, and may be an aspect of Kali. Heals diseases like chicken pox, smallpox, and cholera.
Marie-Aimée	Caribbean, Martinique	Goddess of health, healing, and fatal diseases, causing or curing.

NAME	CULTURE	DESCRIPTION
Mastor-ava, Azer-ava	Europe, Finno-Ugric, Erya, Moksha, Mordvin	Earth mother goddess of healing, health, agriculture, and the harvest.
Medica, Minerva Medica	Mediterranean, Roman	The goddess Minerva in her role as the patroness of physicians.
Medicine Buddhas, Abheda, Mi-Che-Pa, Mi-P'yed	Tibet, Buddhist	Appear in groups of eight or nine, wearing monks' robes, and are said to have supernatural wisdom.
Meditrina	Mediterranean, Roman	Goddess of health, healing magick and charms, herbal preparations, and wine.
Meme	Africa, Uganda	The creator of life and goddess of health, shamanic healing, teaching the healing arts, longevity, joy, harvest, and ghosts. Symbols: beer and corn.
Merit Ptah	Africa, Egyptian	Deified mortal physician who lived ca. 2700 BCE in Egypt; the first female doctor recorded in history, and perhaps the first named woman in science. Her name means Beloved of the God Ptah.
Miach	Europe, Celtic	Son of DIAN CECHT. Brilliant surgeon. 365 different healing herbs grew on his grave.
Mina Koya	North America, Pueblo	Goddess of salt, cleansing, protecting, preserving, health, healing power, blessing, and weather. Symbol: salt. Celebrated in the autumn.
Mirahuato	South America, Peru, Huarochiri District	Goddess of health and healing.
Miritatsiec	North America, Plains, Crow	Moon goddess of the night, healing, hunting, and wild animals, who teaches the healing arts and aids those who are suffering or lost.

Additional Gods and Goddesses

NAME	CULTURE	DESCRIPTION
Mokosh	Europe, Slavic	Goddess of spinning, rain, abundance, health, and the healing of the handicapped. Symbols: breast-shaped stones.
Momoy	North America, California, Chumash	Goddess of ancestors, shamans, immortality, healing, magick, knowledge, widows and foster parents, adoption, social rules, and tradition.
Mother Of All Eagles	North America, Native American	Represents health, healing, power, destiny, freedom, perspective, vision, air, and movement. Symbols: feathers.
Mukuru	Africa, Hereroan	God of healing, creation, protection, and rain. Name means All Alone.
Mulhalmoni	Asia, Korea	Water goddess who protects the eyes and heals blindness or any eye disease. Likes offerings of rice and coins.
Mullo, Mars Mullo	Europe, Celtic, Gaul	God who specializes in healing diseases of the eye, though he heals other organs as well. Had many shrines and temples, and urban sanctuaries. Name means Mule.
Nalygyr-aissyt-khotun	Europe and Asia, Slavic, Siberia, Yakut	Benevolent goddess of childbirth, the sky, and the heavens.
Nana Buluku	Africa, Haiti, the Fon	Androgynous deity of herbs and medicine, as well as supreme deity.
Nanna, Nina	Mesopotamia, Sumer	Goddess of herbs, healing, magickm, the moon, dreams, and civilization. Called The Holy One of Many Names.
Namtar, Namtaru, Namtara	Mesopotamia)	Minor god of death and disease, and the messenger of An, Ereshkigal, and Nergal. Name means Destiny, or Fate.
Nastasija	Europe, Slavic, Russia, Mordvin	Goddess of sleep, health, and healing.

183

NAME	CULTURE	DESCRIPTION
Neith, Neit, Net, Nit	Africa, Egyptian	Mother goddess, of war, the hunt, healing, herbs, medicine, ritual, and much more. Name means The Huntress, and she is called Opener of the Ways. Her priests were physicians.
Nejma	Africa, Morocco	Goddess of health and healing, protection, courage, and organization. She oversees and organizes all other health and healing spirits, warding off spring colds and other maladies. Goddess of healthcare workers. Lives in a grotto. Symbols: caverns and water.
Nerthus	Europe, Teutonic	Earth goddess of health, spring, energy, peace, and prosperity. Symbols: fire, chariot, and soil.
Nikko-Bosatsu	Asia, Japan, Buddhist	Bodhisattva of good health and sunshine.
Nina	Mesopotamia	Mother goddess of herbal healing, health, herb magick, mediation, dreams, cooperation, magick, and civilization. Protects well-being over the winter.
Ninazu	Mesopotmia, Sumer	Benevolent god of healing and the underworld. The consort of **Ninsutu**, one of the deities born to relieve the illness of Enki. The patron deity of the city of Eshnunna.
Ningishzida	Mesopotamia	God (though sometimes said to be female) of medicine and the underworld. Lord of the Good Tree. Occasionally shown as a serpent with a human head. Associated with Ningishzida is the earliest known symbol of snakes twining around a rod or staff, predating the Rod of Asclepius and the Caduceus of Hermes by more than a thousand years.

Additional Gods and Goddesses

NAME	CULTURE	DESCRIPTION
Niniano	Pacific, Polynesia, Marquesas Islands	Goddess of healing, fishing, water creatures, family, tribe, and community.
Ninsu-Utud, Ninsutu	Mesopotamia, Babylonia, Sumer	Goddess of healing, especially aching teeth. One of the deities born to relieve the illness of Enki.
Ninti	Mesopotamia, Sumer	One of eight goddesses of healing created by NINHURSAG; specializing in the ribs.
Nintil	Mesopotamia, Sumer	One of eight goddesses of healing created by NINHURSAG.
Nintud, Innini, Ninanna, Nintu, Belit, Belit-Ilani	Mesopotamia, Sumer	Mother earth goddess of childbirth
Ninurta, Ningirsu, Ninib, Ninip	Mesopotamia	God of healing, hunting and war, and the South Wind. Battles monsters and carries a sword, mace, or bow and arrows.
Nirriti	India, Hindu	Old woman goddess, who takes on the burdens of the world, including disease. Dresses all in black. Patron of the poor as long as they attempt to live a good life.
No'oma Cawaneyung	North America, Northeast, Lenape	Goddess of healing, medicinal plants, and the directions. Grandmother of the South.
Nuit, Nut	Africa, Egyptian	Goddess of the night sky, air, health, and the four winds. Symbols: turquoise, stars, wind, musk, cows, and pots.
Numod-emei	Europe and Asia, Slavic, Siberia, Yukaghir	Goddess of the home, health, and healing.
Nundã	North America, Southeast, Cherokee	Goddess of the sun, the day, healing, time, calendars, and death. She can cause fevers and headaches, and heal them.

Section II, Part 2

NAME	CULTURE	DESCRIPTION
Oki Tsu Hime	Asia, Japan, Shinto	Goddess of kitchens, food, family, health, emotional warmth, fire, and kinship. Symbol: pot of boiling water.
Okuni-Nushino-Mikoto, Yachiholo-No Kami, Okuninushi	Asia, Japan	God of medicine, sorcery, cunning, self-realization, and magick, called the God of Eight Thousand Spears. Name means Great Land Master.
Onenha	North America, Northeast, Seneca	Corn goddess of healing, agriculture, knowledge, and the Corn Harvest Ceremony.
Orbona	Mediterranean, Roman	Goddess of healing and safety for children.
Orehu	Caribbean, Guyana, Arawak	Goddess of health and healing; called The Water Mother.
Orunmila, Fa, Gbaye-Gborun, Ifa	Africa, Yoruba	God of healers, childbirth, the sky, and divination; physician and herbalist; patron of health clinics; divine messenger of the gods.
Osanyin	Africa	God of curative medicine and divination.
Oshun	Africa, Yoruba; Caribbean, Brazil, West Indies, Cuba, Haiti	Goddess of fresh water, health, healing, love, sexuality, beauty, and wealth.
Paean, Paeëon, Paieon, Paeon, Paion	Mediterannean, Greek	Wise physician of the gods, who knows the remedies for all illnesses, and brings healing and relief from pain.
Pakwaekasiasit	North America, Northeast, Penobscot	Goddess of medicinal herbs. Arrow-head Finger.
Panglang	Southeast Asia, Philippines, Bukidnon	Goddess of unborn children, pregnancy, and childbirth. Patron of midwives.
Pasowee, Buffalo Old Woman	North America, Plains, Kiowa	Buffalo Woman, goddess of health, healing, medicine, knowledge, hunting, wild animals, and home and shelter.

Additional Gods and Goddesses

NAME	CULTURE	DESCRIPTION
Patecatl	Central America, Aztec	God of fertility and healing, associated with peyote and the pulque root.
The Perit	Europe, Slavic, Albania	Mountain spirits of health, healing, earth, nature, time, and justice. They dress all in white.
Perun, Pyerun, Piorun, Peron, Perunu, Perkaunas	Europe, Slavic	Supreme creator god of thunder and lightning, purification, fertility, defense against illness, and much more. Name means Thunder.
Phoebus	Mediterranean, Roman	Roman equivalent of Apollo, god of medicine, the healing rays of the sun, and protection against plague.
Pi-Hsia Yuan-Chin, Sheng-Mu, Yu Nu, T'ien Hsien	Asia, China, Taoist	Goddess of childbirth, protection of mothers, and health and good fortune for newborn children. She has six assistant goddesses, and is called the Princess of the Blue and Purple Clouds.
Piluitus, Pilnitis, Pilwittus	Europe, Slavic, Latvia, Lithuania, Prussia	Goddess or possibly god, of healing, fertility, agriculture, and the harvest.
Pinga	North America, Arctic, Caribou Inuit	Goddess of fertility, medicine, reincarnation, and the hunt. Also guided the souls of the dead to the underworld. Guardian of animals. Name means The One Who is [Up On] High.
Po Yan Dari	Southeast Asia, Cambodia	Goddess of death and disease, but also health and healing; can be found in caves—leave offerings there.
Purt-kūva	Europe, Slavic, Russia, Cheremis	Goddess of the household, fate, luck, healing, and wealth. Name means House Woman. She is temperamental if not given offerings of beer and bread.

Section II, Part 2

NAME	CULTURE	DESCRIPTION
Quetzalcoatl, Kukulcan (Maya), Ometecutli and others	Central America, Aztec, Toltec, Maya	Supreme god who ruled medicine and the healing arts, fertility, wealth, farming, and much more. His name means Feathered Serpent, and he appears as a bearded old man in a long robe. His double, twin, or companion is Xolotl, a dog with raggedy ears.
Rainbow Snake, Julunggul	Australia, Aboriginal	Goddess of health, fertility, rain, magickal healing arts, children, life, beauty, joy, and protecting sacred traditions. Symbols: rainbows, rainwater, flowers, pearls.
Rauni, Maan-Eno, Ravdna, Roonikka	Europe, Finnish	Forest Mother and goddess of thunder, the mountain ash, childbirth, and ease from pain.
Red-spider-woman	North America, Plains, Pawnee	Goddess of healing, insects, and farming, especially beans, squash, and corn—the "three sisters" of southwest farming.
Rosmerta	Europe, Celtic	Goddess of prosperity, sacred springs, healing shrines, trade, and abundance. Carries a bag of food or a basket of fruit.
Rua hine metua	Pacific, Polynesia, New Zealand, Maori	Goddess of protection, joy, inner peace, emotional healing, and order. Called Old Mother.
Rugaba, Ruhanga, Kazooba, Mukameiguru	Africa, Uganda, Ankorean	God of creation, the sun and sky, life, fertility, health, healing, sickness, death, and judgment.
Sakarabru	Africa, Guinea, Agni	God of medicine, justice and retribution, and darkness, who sometimes appears as a ball of maize.
Salema and Sakia	Middle East, Arab	Gods of health and rain, respectively.
Salus	Mediterranean, Roman	Goddess of health, public welfare, and prosperity. "salutary" derives from her name.

Additional Gods and Goddesses

NAME	CULTURE	DESCRIPTION
Sarakka	Europe, Finno-Ugric, Lapland, Saami	Goddess of childbirth and the home, the hearth, spinning, hunting, and wild animals.
Savitri	India, Hindu	Goddess of healing, long life, immortality, sunrise, sunset, night, and rest. Shown as a golden-haired goddess in a chariot drawn by two bright horses.
Senhora Ana	South America, Brazil, Belem	Goddess of health, healing, the elderly, altruism, and humility.
Sequana	Europe, Celtic	River goddess of good health, luck, youthfulness, and movement. Stands in a duck-shaped boat. Associated with April showers.
Serqet, Selqet, Selket, Serket, Selcis	Africa, Egypt	Goddess of healing venomous stings and bites, as well as fertility, medicine, magic, animals, and nature. She also protects the living and the dead from evil. Her name may mean She Who Causes the Throat to Breathe. Shown as a scorpion or a woman with a scorpion on her head.
Shadrapha, Shadrafa, Shed the Healer	Mediterranean, Phoenicia	God of healing, and conqueror of evil. He stands on a lion, under a sun symbol.
Shen Nung	Asia, China	God of medicine, pharmacy, and agriculture.
Shimhanada, Lokeswara	India, Buddhist	An aspect of Avalokitesvara; he is healer of all diseases. Wears a tiger skin, sits on a lion, and holds a trident with a white snake wrapped around it.
Sinnilktok	North America, Arctic, Baffin Land Inuit	Very benevolent goddess of health, healing, domesticated animals, food, who appears as a creature who is half human and half dog.
Soma, Amrit, Amrita, Chandra,	India and Persia, Hindu	Healing god connected with soma, the drink of the gods. God of herbs, flowing waters, inspiration, wealth, and the moon. Shown as a

189

NAME	CULTURE	DESCRIPTION
Haoma, Indu, and others		celestial bull, a youth, or a bird. His symbol is the silver crescent.
Sopona, Shapona, Saponna, Babalu Aye, Omolu	Africa and the Caribbean, Yoruba, Candomblé	God of smallpox, contagious disease in general, skin disease, and insanity; he can inflict or cure them. His name must not be spoken aloud, to avoid invoking the disease. He is linked with certain beetles, flies, mosquitoes and black butterflies.
Suku-Na-Biko	Japan, Shinto	God, chief of the medicine deities.
Sulis, Sul, Sulivia, Sel, Sullis	Europe, Celtic	Goddess of sacred wells and springs, water, healing, eye health and vision, blessings, and community. Also a sun goddess with ever-burning fires in her temples. Shown wearing a heavy black cloak and a bearskin hat. Symbols: water, fire, bears, owls, and wheat cakes.
Sung-Tzu-Naing-Naing, His Wang Mu, Wang Mu Niang Niang Weiwobo	Asia, China	Goddess of healing, fecundity, and newborn children. Cures disease and protects the Herb of Immortality. Shown with a baby in her arms. Queen of the West. Likes rattles, incense, and firecrackers.
Suonetar	Europe, Finno-Ugric, Finland, Saami	Goddess of health and healing, and especially the veins, immortality, and magick.
Ta-Bitjet	Africa, Egyptian	Scorpion goddess whose blood is a universal remedy for all poisons.
Takanakapsaluk	North America, Arctic, Iglulik Inuit	Arctic sea goddess of personal health, healing, purification, strength, thankfulness, luck, hunting, wild animals, justice and judgment, and caring for the spirits of the dead.
Tamayorihime	Asia, Japan	Goddess of the sea, water, cleansing, birth, and children. She ensures a speedy, safe delivery for pregnant women.

Additional Gods and Goddesses

NAME	CULTURE	DESCRIPTION
Tamra	India, Hindu	The ancestress of all birds and goddess of health, longevity, relationships, devotion, nature, earth, air, and communications from the gods. Symbols: feathers and birdseed.
Tcakwena Okya	North America, Soutwest, Zuni	Goddess or kachina of fertility, childbirth, protection of children, and longevity.
Temazcalteci	Central America, Aztec	Goddess of health, banishing illness, medicinal herbs, healing amulets, and water. Name means Grandmother of the Sweat Bath. Especially powerful in Autumn.
Teteoinnan, Teteoninnan	Central America, Mexico, Aztec	Goddess of healers, midwives, nature, the Earth, and fertility. Called The Mother of Sacred Ones.
Te vahine nui tahu ra'i	Pacific, Polynesia, Raiatea	Goddess of healing after serious sickness, protection, fire, fire-walkers, and magick.
Thoth, Aah, Tehuti, And Others	Africa, Egyptian	God of medicine, astronomy, time, magick, and much more. Cures poisons. Shown as an ibis, an ibis-headed man, or a baboon.
Three-Legged Ass	Middle East, Persia	Benevolent god who destroys disease and pests. As large as a mountain, with three giant feet, six eyes, and nine mouths.
Thrita, Faridun, Thraetana and more	Middle East, Persia	Healing god who drives away serious disease and death. Patron of healing plants, and relieves itches, fevers, and incontinence.
Tlazolteotl	Central America, Mexico, Aztec	Goddess of sexuality, purification, midwives, healers, weavers, household affairs, immortality, magick, and time. The "Filth Goddess," who takes on herself the sins of those confessing to her.
Tlitcaplitana	North America, Northwest, Bella Coola	Goddess of the sky, the heavens, healing, knowledge, and magick. Descended from the heavens, to share health, healing, and the

191

NAME	CULTURE	DESCRIPTION
		secret knowledge and chants. She could sing people to health with her beautiful voice, though not physically attractive—she had a big nose.
Tozi, Toci, Teteoinnan, Cihuatzin	Central America, Aztec	Mother of the gods, healing, midwives, purification and sweat baths, and the healing powers of nature. Patron of midwives, doctors, and surgeons. Her festival honored women healers. Name means Our Grandmother.
Tu-Njami	Asia, Siberia	Goddess of purification, healing, childbirth, and protection of women and families. Name means Mother Fire. A young, naked girl.
Tzapotla Tenan, Tzaputaltena	Central America, Mexico, Aztec	Goddess of herbal healing, treating skin diseases, and sore throats.
Uli, Ouli	Pacific, Polynesia, Hawaii	Goddess of life, death, healing, magick, and curses.
Umina	South America, Ecuador	God of medicine, represented by a large emerald.
Unkatahe	North America, Native American	Water deity, depicted as a sacred serpent. He or she has power over disease and the transmigration of souls, and is shown with crescent horns representing the moon, as well as circles and spiral designs.
Uzume	Asia, Japan	Goddess of health, happiness, and the dance. Her stream flows with blessed healing water. Name means Whirling, and she is called Heaven's Forthright Female.
Vaidya-Nath	India, Hindu	A healing aspect of Shiva; Lord of the Knowing Ones, or Lord of the Physicians.
Ved'ma	Europe, Slavic	Goddess of magick, witchcraft, medicinal plants, rain and storms. Keeper of the sacred water of life and death.

Additional Gods and Goddesses

NAME	CULTURE	DESCRIPTION
Verminus	Mediterannean, Roman	God who protects cattle from disease.
The Vila, Willi, Judy, Samovila	Europe, Slavic, Serbia, Slovenia	Shape-shifting forest spirits of nature, earth, healing, agriculture, knowledge, wealth, justice, and ceremonies.
Waiora, Waiola, Vai-Ola	Polynesian	Goddess of health, who had a sacred well that could cure all disease. Water of Life.
Widapokwi	North America, Southwest, Yavapai	Goddess of health, healing, medicine songs, and protection from storms and whirlwinds.
The Wilden Wip	Europe, Germany	Female forest spirits of healing, magick, and sexuality; they like human men.
!Xu, !Xuba, !Xo, !Xoba	Africa, Bushman	Omnipotent, benevolent supreme sky god who is invoked in illness, for rain, and prior to traveling or hunting. Calls magicians to their vocation, and gathers the souls of the dead.
Yakushi-Nyorai, Bhaishajya (Hindu)	Asia, Japan, Buddhist	God, Giver of Cures, one of the six Buddhas of meditation.
Yamantaka, Manjusri, and more	India, Tibet, Buddhist, Hindu	God, Destroyer of Death, shown with the head of a bull, a third eye, wearing a crown of skulls.
Yanauluha	North America, Southwest, Zuni	God of healing, agriculture, animal husbandry, knowledge, and civilization. Great Medicine Man.
Yao-Shih	Asia, China	Master of Healing, and Lord of Psychic Abilities.
Yegiled-emei	Europe, Slavic, Siberia, Yukaghir	Fire goddess of healing.
Yo-Wang, Yo-Shi-Wang Fo	Asia, China, Buddhist	God of healing and medicines.
Zarya	Europe, Slavic	Goddess of the healing waters, sacred springs, and holy wells.
Ziva, Siva, Zywie	Europe, Slavic	Goddess of life, health, healing, longevity, regeneration, and rebirth. Her name means Living.

Part 3
Planetary and Zodiac Gods and Goddesses

While not all of the deities listed here are specifically known as healing deities, each one of these may be able to influence the healing of the part of the body corresponding to the planet or sign with which they are associated.

PLANETS/SIGNS	PART OF BODY	DEITIES
Sun	General vitality, heart, spine	Sol, Aelectrona, Amaterasu, Amun, Apollo, Astarte, Athena, Bast, Belenos, Eos, Erzulie, Grannus, Griane, Helios, Inanna, Inti, Ishtar, Isis, Lugh, Ra, Ri Gong Tai Yang Xing Jun, Saule, Sekhmet, Shams/Shamsun, Sulis, Surya, The Adityas, Tonatiuh, Wadjet
Moon	Digestive system, stomach, lymphatic system, female organs	Luna, Achelois, Ala, Alignak, Anumati, Arianrhod, Artemis, Avatea, Bahloo, Chandra, Chang'e, Chang Xi, Chup Kamui, Coniraya, Coyolxauhqui, Diana, Elatha, Fati, Gleti, Haliya, Hekate, Iah, Igaluk, Ilargi, Isis, Ixbalanque, Jarilo, Kalfu, Kaskuh, Khonsu, Kusuh, Kuu, Losna, Mama Killa, Máni, Mano, Marama, Mawi, Men, Meness, Napir, Neith, Nepthys, Nikkal, Phoebe, Selene, Sin, Susanoo, Ta'lab, Thoth, Trivia, Tsukuyomi, Wadd, Yarikh

PLANETS/ SIGNS	PART OF BODY	DEITIES
Mercury	Central nervous system, brain, hands, five senses, thyroid	Mercury, Hermes
Venus	Throat, kidneys, ovaries, thymus, sense of touch	Venus, Aphrodite
Earth	All of the body	Gaia, Ceres, Coatlicue, Demeter, Geb, Ki, Mater Tellus, Mati Syra Zemlya, Ninhursag, Pachamama, Parvati
Mars	Head, muscles, adrenals, senses of smell and taste	Mars, Ares, Athena, Bellona, Scathach
Jupiter	Growth, thighs, feet, liver, pituitary	Jove, Vejovis, Zeus, JHVH
Saturn	Skin, hair, bones, teeth, immunity, spleen	Saturn, Kronos
Uranus	Neural activity, parathyroid, aura	Uranus
Neptune	Psychic healing, pineal	Neptune, Aphrodite, Manannan, Poseidon, Sedna, Tiamat
Pluto	Metabolism, elimination, pancreas	Pluto, Hades, Hekate, Hel, Persephone, chthonic gods and goddesses

Aries	Head, brain, face, eyes	Ares, Mars, Khnum
Taurus	Throat, neck, vocal chords, thyroid	Osiris, Hathor, Hera, Venus
Gemini	Nervous system, brain, lungs, shoulders, arms, hands	Janus, Apollo, Mercury, Thoth
Cancer	Chest, alimentary canal, chest, breasts	Artemis, Diana, Dionysus, Khephri, Khonsu
Leo	Chest, spine, upper back, heart	Helios, Apollo, Hoor, Khuit, Ra
Virgo	Nervous system, digestive system, intestines, spleen	Isis, Ceres, Demeter, Kore, Mercury, Persephone

PLANETS/ SIGNS	PART OF BODY	DEITIES
Libra	Lumbar spine, kidneys, buttocks, skin	Themis, Maat, Venus
Scorpio	Reproductive system, excretory system, large intestine	Vulcan, Hephaestus, Pluto, Ptah, Set
Sagittarius	Liver, hips, thighs, sciatic nerve	Jupiter, Chiron, Nepthys
Capricorn	Skeletal system, joints, especially knees	Bacchus, Khem, Kronos, Min, Pan, Saturn
Aquarius	Circulatory system, ankles	Juno, Ahephi, Ganymede, Uranus
Pisces	Lymphatic system, fat, feet, toes	Neptune, Anubis, Poseidon

SECTION THREE
Appendices

Appendix A
Cross-Reference by Specialty

SPECIALTY

Featured Deities	Additional Deities
Abortion/Termination of pregnancy	
	Kapo
Abuse	
Bona Dea	
Eshmun	
Acupuncture	
Chinese Deities:	
Wang Wei	
Alcohol Abuse	
Sekhmet	
Anesthesia	
	Anubis
Anger management	
	Kamrusepas
Animal health	
	Damona
	Hertha
	Yanauluha
Ayurvedic Medicine	
Dhanvantari	
Battle injuries	
Airmed	
Birth/Childbirth	
Anahita	Carmentis
Artemis	Ixazalvoh
Brigit	Kapo
Eileithyia	Nintud

SPECIALTY

Featured Deities	Additional Deities
Birth/Childbirth, cont'd	
Eir	Orunmila
Haumea	Pi-Hsia Yuan-Chin
Iaso	
Isis	Rauni
Ixchel	Tamayorihime
Kwan Yin	Tu-Njami
Mati Syra Zemlya	
Ninhursag	
Nodens	
Tawaret	
Blood disorders	
Dhanvantari	
Erinle	
Bones, disease/injury	
Ebisu	
Sekhmet	
Breastfeeding	
Isis	
Ninhursag	
Tawaret	
Breathing	
	Serqet
Burns	
Grannus	
Cattle	
	Verminus

201

Appendix A

SPECIALTY

Featured Deities	Additional Deities
Chicken pox	
	Mari
Childhood Diseases/Injuries	
Ebisu	Carmentis
Eileithyia	Kiri Amma
Eshmun	Mama Cocha
Isis	Orbona
Kwan Yin	Rainbow Snake
Tawaret	Tamayorihime
Chiropractic	
Chiron	
Cholera	
	Mari
Cleansing/Purification	
Brigit	Fons
Ixchel	Ganga
Kupala/	Huchi
Kupalo	Izu No Me Mo
Kwan Yin	Kami
Mama Cocha	Kamrusepas
	Mina Koya
	Perun
	Takanakapsaluk
	Tamayorihime
	Tozi
	Tu-Njami
Contagious Diseases, Epidemics, and Plague	
Apollo	Sopona
Babalú-Ayé	Phoebus
Eir	
Hygieia	
Mati Syra	
Zemlya	
Sitala	
Vejovis	
Contagious Diseases, protection from	
Artemis	

SPECIALTY

Featured Deities	Additional Deities
Convalescence, Recovery	
Iaso	
Telesphoros	
(see Asclepius)	
Depression (see also Mental/Emotional Illness)	
Beiwe	
Fufluns	
Kwan Yin	
Sitala	
Digestive Problems	
Carna	
Diagnostics	
Grannus	
Podaleirios	
(see Asclepius)	
Mati Syra	
Zemlya	
Nehalennia	
Drugs, Pharmaceuticals	
	Imhotep
	Shen Nung
Exercise/Fitness/Strength	
Artemis	
Herakles	
Sekhmet	
Vejovis	
Eyes/Eye afflictions	
Apollo	Caolainn
Brigit	Mother of All Eagles
	Mulhalmoni
	Mullo

SPECIALTY

Featured Deities	Additional Deities
Fatigue/Low Energy/Energy Body	
Borvo	Lada
Chinese Deities (look for qi)	Nerthus
Gula	
Heka	
Herakles	
Fertility	
Anahita	Bast
Artemis	Carmentis
Beiwe	Damara
Bona Dea	Epona
Brigit	Famien
Eileithyia	Gefn
Haumea	Gunnloed
Herakles	Habondia
Isis	Hertha
Ixchel	Haoma
Kwan Yin	Jun Ti
Mami Wata	Patecatl
Mati Syra Zemlya (men)	Perun
	Pinga
	Quetzalcoatl
Nehalennia	Rainbow Snake
Ninhursag	Rugaba
Shaushka	Serqet
Sirona	Sung-Tzu-Naing-Naing
Tawaret	
Fevers/Malaria	
Gula	Febris
Sitala	Mahalbiya
	Thrita
Flu/Influenza	
Babalú-Ayé	

SPECIALTY

Featured Deities	Additional Deities
Handicaps	
	Mokosh
Health in Autumn	
	Temazcalteci
Health in Winter	
	Nina
Healthcare Workers/Medical Administration/Health Clinics	
	Nejma
	Orunmila
Heart	
Carna	
Herbs/Herbalism/ Herbal Healing	
Airmed	Aja
Angitia	Ameretat
Babalú-Ayé	Dziwozony
Bona Dea	Bai Zu Shen
Chinese Deities	Buschfrauen
	Buschgrossmutter
Dhanvantari	Circe
Erinle	Haoma
Haumea	Hexe
Kupala/ Kupalo	Imaymana Viracocha
Ninhursag	Imhotep
Sitala	Kaya-Nu-Hima
	Loco
	Meditrina
	Miach
	NanaBuluku
	Neith
	Nina
	Orunmila
	Soma
	Sung-Tzu-Naing-Naing
	Temazcalteci
	Thrita

203

Appendix A

SPECIALTY	
Featured Deities	Additional Deities

HIV/AIDS
  Babalú-Ayé
Hospitalization
                      Anubis
Hygiene/Sanitation
  Chinese Deities
  Erzulie
  Hygieia
Incontinence
                      Thrita
Inflammation
  Gula
Injury
  Apollo
  Ebisu
  Isis (critical injury)
  Kumugwe
  Nodens
  Sekhmet
  Sirona
Internal Medicine
  Chinese Deities: Sun
  Simiao
Internal Organs
  Chinese Deities
Itching
                      Thrita
Leg Injury or Illness
Leprosy
  Babalú-Ayé
  Brigit
LGBT Health issues (see also HIV/AIDS)
  Erinle
  Shaushka

SPECIALTY	
Featured Deities	Additional Deities

Life-threatening Illness
  Asclepius
  Pajau Yan
Light Therapy
  Apollo
  Grannus
Liver
  Carna
Longevity
                      Ahurani
                      Chin Mu
                      Fukurokujin
                      Hertha
                      Jun Ti
                      Meme
                      Savitri
                      Tamra
Lungs
  Carna
Massage, therapeutic
  Chiron
Mental/Emotional Illness
  Beiwe   Sopona
  Artemis
  Fufluns
  Hygieia
  Kwan Yin
  Mama Cocha
  Menrva
  Nodens
Midwives
  Eileithyia   Tozi
  Ixchel
  Mati Syra Zemlya
Music Therapy
  Apollo
  Chiron

Cross-Reference by Specialty

SPECIALTY

Featured Deities	Additional Deities
Nature Therapy	
Artemis	
Haumea	
Mati Syra	
Zemlya	
Newborns	
	Rauni
	Sung-Tzu-Naing-Naing
Nightmares	
Carna	
Sitala	
Nutrition for Healing	
Haumea	
Mama Cocha	
Mati Syra	
Zemlya	
Nehalennia	
Ninhursag	
Pain management	
Kwan Yin	Epione
	Imhotep
	Paean
	Rauni
Physicians	
Dian Cécht	Medica
Eir	Merit Ptah
Gula	Neith
Sekhmet	Imhotep
Uretsete (medicine men)	Tozi
Poison	
Gula	Thoth
	Ta-Bitjet
Pregnancy/Maternity	
	Aveta
	Epona
	Kiri Amma
	Pi-Hsia Yuan-Chin

SPECIALTY

Featured Deities	Additional Deities
Pregnancy/Maternity cont'd	
	Tamayorihime
Preventive Medicine	
Hygieia	
Protection from Disease	
Carna	Akerbeltz
	Bast
	Huchi
	Lenus
	Mina Koya
	Perun
Puberty, difficult	
Artemis	
Public Health and Safety	
Endovelicus (see Asclepius)	
Hygieia	
Nehalennia	
Uretsete (for Pueblo peoples)	
Naotste (for non-Pueblo peoples)	
Vejovis	
Relationship Issues	
	Oki Tsu Hime
	Tamra
Ribs	
	Ninti
Scorpion stings	
	Ta-Bitjet
Seasonal Affective Disorder (SAD)	
Beiwe	
Sexual Dysfunction	
Anahita	
Erzulie	
Herakles (men's)	
Isis	

205

Appendix A

SPECIALTY

Featured Deities	Additional Deities
Sexual Dysfunction cont'd	
Ixchel	
Mami Wata	
Shaushka	
Shamanic healing	
Meme	
Skin disease, ulcers, leprosy	
Brigit	Mahalbiya
	Sopona
Sleep disorders	
Imhotep	Ixtlilton
Gula	
Smallpox	
Mari	Sopona
Snakebite	
Angitia	Serqet
	Janguli
Spiritual dis-ease	
Carna	Derzelas
Strength	
Borvo	
Herakles	
Sunstroke	
Apollo	
Grannus	
Sekhmet	
Surgery	
Anubis	
Miach	
Machaon	
Sekhmet	
Chinese, Hua Tuo	
Teeth/Toothache	
	Ahau-Chamahez
	Aibheaog
	Hesy-Ra
	Ninsu-Utud

SPECIALTY

Featured Deities	Additional Deities
Transgender Issues/Sex Change	
Kwan Yin	Bhaishajyaguru
Vermin/Lice/Fleas	
	Three-Legged-Ass
	Verminus
Water Therapy	
Anahita	
Borvo	
Brigit	
Endovelicus (see Asclepius)	
Erinle	
Grannus	
Ixchel	
Mama Cocha	
Mami Wata	
Nehalennia	
Nodens	
Sirona	
Tawaret	
Women Healers	
Eir	Tozi
	Merit Ptah
Women's Health	
Bast	Bebhionn
Eir	Chin Mu
Isis	Damia
Ixchel	Merit Ptah
Kwan Yin	Tu-Njami
Mati Syra Zemlya	
Pajau Yan	
Youth	
	Iovantucarus

206

Appendix B
Cross-Reference by Region and Culture

If a certain culture or part of the world resonates with you, you may find this list helpful in finding a deity to work with.

CULTURE	NAME	DESCRIPTION
Africa	Osanyin	God of curative medicine and divination.
Africa and the Caribbean, Yoruba, Candomblé	Sopona, Shapona, Saponna, Babalu Aye, Omolu	God of smallpox, contagious disease in general, skin disease, and insanity; he can inflict or cure them. His name must not be spoken aloud, to avoid invoking the disease. He is linked with certain beetles, flies, mosquitoes and black butterflies.
Africa, Bushman	!Xu, !Xuba, !Xo, !Xoba	Omnipotent, benevolent supreme sky god who is invoked in illness, for rain, and prior to traveling or hunting. Calls magicians to their vocation, and gathers the souls of the dead.
Africa, Egyptian	Amenhetep	God of healing.
	Anubis, Anpu, Sekhem Em Pet	Jackal-headed god of funeral rites and the underworld, protector and judge of the dead, anesthetics, hospital stays, medicine, surgery, justice, truth, wisdom, and much more.

Appendix B

CULTURE	NAME	DESCRIPTION
Africa, Egyptian	Bast, Bastet, Pasht	Cat-headed goddess of the gentle sunlight, the moon, fertility, childbirth, protection against disease, healing, joy, dance, music, and more.
	Heka	Featured
	Heqet, Heket, Hekt, Heqt, Heqtit, and more	Goddess of primordial waters, fertility, childbirth, and regeneration. Giver of life. Shown as a frog.
	Hesy-Ra	An official and priest of Egypt, during the reign of Pharoah (and physician) Djoser. The first person in the history of that ancient land to be recognized as a professional dentist. Deified after death.
	Imhotep, I-Em-Hetep, Iemhetep, Imhetep, Imuthes (Greek)	An Egyptian polymath, skilled in medicine, engineering, architecture, philosophy and more. Lived in the 27th century BCE, he was a priest of Ra. Deified 2,000 years after his death. God of medicine, healing, physicians, herbs, drugs, sleep to heal suffering and pain, learning, and more. Name means The One Who Comes in Peace.
	Isis	Featured
	Khensu, Khonsu, Aa, Khons	God of healing, regeneration, and the moon. His name means Traveler.
	Merit Ptah	Deified mortal physician who lived ca. 2700 BCE in Egypt; the first female doctor recorded in history, and perhaps the first named woman in science. Her name means Beloved of the God Ptah.

Region and Culture

CULTURE	NAME	DESCRIPTION
Africa, Egyptian	Neith, Neit, Net, Nit	Mother goddess, of war, the hunt, healing, herbs, medicine, ritual, and much more. Name means The Huntress, and she is called Opener of the Ways. Her priests were physicians.
	Nuit, Nut	Goddess of the night sky, air, health, and the four winds. Symbols: turquoise, stars, wind, musk, cows, and pots.
	Sekhmet	Featured
	Serqet, Selqet, Selket, Serket, Selcis	Goddess of healing venomous stings and bites, as well as fertility, medicine, magic, animals, and nature. She also protects the living and the dead from evil. Her name may mean She Who Causes the Throat to Breathe. Shown as a scorpion or a woman with a scorpion on her head.
	Ta-Bitjet	Scorpion goddess whose blood is a universal remedy for all poisons.
	Tawaret	Featured
	Thoth, Aah, Tehuti, and others	God of medicine, astronomy, time, magick, and much more. Cures poisons. Shown as an ibis, an ibis-headed man, or a baboon.
Africa, Guinea	Famien	God of fertility and good health. Carried one or two knives in a medicine bag.
Africa, Guinea, Agni	Sakarabru	God of medicine, justice and retribution, and darkness, who sometimes appears as a ball of maize.
Africa, Haiti, the Fon	Nana Buluku	Androgynous deity of herbs and medicine, as well as supreme deity.
Africa, Hereroan	Mukuru	God of healing, creation, rain, protection, Means All Alone.

209

Appendix B

CULTURE	NAME	DESCRIPTION
Africa, Housa	Mahalbiya	Goddess who causes skin diseases and ulcers, yet gives the power to heal them to dancers whom she possesses during ritual.
Africa, Morocco	Nejma	Goddess of health and healing, protection, courage, and organization. She oversees and organizes all other health and healing spirits, warding off spring colds and other maladies. Goddess of healthcare workers. Lives in a grotto. Symbols: caverns and water.
Africa, southeastern Nigeria, Efik, Ibibio and Annang people; Americas, Caribbean	Mami Wata	Featured
Africa, Uganda	Meme	The creator of life and goddess of health, shamanic healing, teaching the healing arts, longevity, joy, harvest, and ghosts. Symbols: beer and corn.
Africa, Uganda, Ankorean	Rugaba, Ruhanga, Kazooba, Mukameiguru	God of creation, the sun and sky, life, fertility, health, healing, sickness, death, and judgment.
Africa, Yoruba	Orunmila, Fa, Gbaye-Gborun, Ifa	God of healers, childbirth, the sky, and divination; physician and herbalist; patron of health clinics; divine messenger of the gods.
Africa, Yoruba, and Latin America	Erinle	Featured
Africa, Yoruba; Caribbean, Brazil, West Indies, Cuba, Haiti	Oshun	Goddess of fresh water, health, healing, love, sexuality, beauty, and wealth.
Africa, Yoruba; Caribbean,	Aja	Orisha of the forest and wild animals. She is also patron of

CULTURE	NAME	DESCRIPTION
Santeria		herbal healers, and a teacher to all who practice the healing arts.
Africa: Yoruba, Fon, Ewe; and the Caribbean & Latin America: Santerian, Candomblé, Umbanda and Macumba	Babalú-Ayé	Featured
Asia	Kwan Yin	Featured
Asia, China	Bai Suzhen, Bai Zu Shen	Known as Madame White Snake, White Lady, or the White Maiden. An immortal who can present as a lovely maiden or transform into a huge and powerful snake. In her form as a human woman, she falls in love with a mortal man. Together they open an herbal medicine shop, and become renowned as great healers.
Asia, China	Chin Mu	Goddess of health and long life, femininity, and magick; Queen of the West; an ageless, beautiful woman living in a golden castle. Name means Golden Mother. Symbols: peach, mulberry, cats, and golden objects.
	Chinese Deities of Health and Healing	Featured
	Shen Nung	God of medicine, pharmacy, and agriculture.
	Sung-Tzu-Naing-Naing, His Wang Mu, Wang Mu Niang Niang Weiwobo	Goddess of healing, fecundity, and newborn children. Cures disease and protects the Herb of Immortality. Shown with a baby in her arms. Queen of the West. Likes rattles, incense, and firecrackers.

211

Appendix B

CULTURE	NAME	DESCRIPTION
Asia, China	Yao-Shih	Master of Healing, and Lord of Psychic Abilities.
Asia, China, Buddhism	Jun Ti	Goddess of fertility, long life, wisdom, luck, power, and protection. Lives on Polaris. Symbols: dragons, the sun, the moon, and the numbers three and eighteen.
Asia, China, Buddhist	Yo-Wang, Yo-Shi-Wang Fo	God of healing and medicines.
Asia, China, Taoist	Pi-Hsia Yuan-Chin, Sheng-Mu, Yu Nu, T'ien Hsien	Goddess of childbirth, protection of mothers, and health and good fortune for newborn children. She has six assistant goddesses, and is called the Princess of the Blue and Purple Clouds.
Asia, Indian, Nepalese, Bangladeshi, Pakistani	Sitala	Featured
Asia, Japan	Huchi	Goddess of fire, cleansing, health, protection from disease, energy, light, and the harvest. Her fires cleanse, energize, and protect.
	Izu No Me Mo Kami	Goddess of purification, cleansing, health, mediation, and rites of purification with water or fire.
	Okuni-Nushino-Mikoto, Yachiholo-No Kami, Okuninushi	God of medicine, sorcery, cunning, self-realization, and magick, called the God of Eight Thousand Spears. Name means Great Land Master.
	Tamayorihime	Goddess of the sea, water, cleansing, birth, and children. She ensures a speedy, safe delivery for pregnant women.
	Uzume	Goddess of health, happiness, and the dance. Her stream flows with blessed healing water.

CULTURE	NAME	DESCRIPTION
		Uzume means Whirling, and she is called Heaven's Forthright Female.
Asia, Japan, Buddhist	Binzuru, Binzuku	Originally mortal, deified because of miraculous abilities to heal the sick.
	Ebisu	Featured
	Fukurokujin	One of the seven deities of luck, the god of health and longevity. Shown with a stork, a cane, and a Book of Fate.
	Nikko-Bosatsu	Bodhisattva of good health and sunshine.
	Yakushi-Nyorai, Bhaishajya (Hindu)	God, Giver of Cures, one of the six Buddhas of meditation.
Asia, Japan, Shinto	Oki Tsu Hime	Goddess of kitchens, food, family, health, emotional warmth, fire, and kinship. Symbol: pot of boiling water.
	Suku-Na-Biko	God, chief of the medicine deities.
Asia, Korea	Mulhalmoni	Water goddess who protects the eyes and heals blindness or any eye disease. Likes offerings of rice and coins.
Asia, Middle East, Persia	Ameretat, Amardad, Amererat, Murdad	God of all green plants, health, long life.
	Anahita	Featured
Asia, Siberia	Tu-Njami	Goddess of purification, healing, childbirth, and protection of women and families. Name means Mother Fire. Looked like a young, naked girl.
Australia, Aboriginal	Rainbow Snake, Julunggul	Goddess of health, fertility, rain, magickal healing arts, children, life, beauty, joy, and protecting sacred traditions. Symbols: rainbows, rainwater, flowers, pearls.

Appendix B

CULTURE	NAME	DESCRIPTION
Caribbean, Guyana, Arawak	Orehu	Goddess of health and healing; called The Water Mother.
Caribbean, Haiti, Dahhomey	Erzulie	Featured
Caribbean, Haiti, Taino	Guabonito	Sea goddess of medicines, health, healing, and ceremonies.
Caribbean, Martinique	Marie-Aimée	Goddess of health, healing, and fatal diseases, which she can cause or cure.
Caribbean, Vodun	Loco, Loko	The loa of healers and plants, particularly trees. A Rada (benevolent) Loa. He and his wife **Ayizan** are believed to be the first priest (houngan) and priestess (mambo), guardians of initiation and the correct rites.
Central America, Aztec	Ixtlilton	God of healing and medicine, called The Little Black One. Thought to reside in an obsidian mask that has the power to bring peaceful sleep to children in their beds. The brother of Macuilxochitl, the god of well-being or good luck.
Central America, Aztec	Patecatl	God of fertility and healing, associated with peyote and the pulque root.
	Temazcalteci	Goddess of health, banishing illness, medicinal herbs, healing amulets, and water. Name means Grandmother of the Sweat Bath. Especially powerful in Autumn.
	Tozi, Toci, Teteoinnan, Cihuatzin	Mother of the gods, healing, midwives, purification and sweat baths, and the healing powers of nature. Patron of midwives, doctors, and surgeons. Her festival honored women healers. Name means Our Grandmother.

Region and Culture

CULTURE	NAME	DESCRIPTION
Central America, Aztec, Toltec, Maya	Quetzalcoatl, Kukulcan (Maya), Ometecutli and others	Supreme god who ruled medicine and the healing arts, fertility, wealth, farming, and much more. His name means Feathered Serpent, and he appears as a bearded old man in a long robe. His double, twin, or companion is Xolotl, a dog with raggedy ears.
Central America, Guatemala, Chorti	Ah Uaynih	Goddess of health, healing; and restful sleep for males.
Central America, Mayan	Ahau-Chamahez	Lord of the Magic Tooth, god of medicine.
	Cit-Bolon-Tum	God of medicine, called Boar of the Nine Tusks. His treatments involve nine precious stones.
	Itzamna, Itzmatul, Izamna and many more	God of healing, the sky, creation, writing, and fertile fields. Can bring the dead back to life. Shown with a red hand.
	Ixazalvoh, Ixzaluoh	Goddess of healing, childbirth, sexuality, weaving, and prophecy.
	Ixchel	Featured
	Kinich Ahau, Kinish-Kakimo	God of healing, medicine, and the sun. His name means The Lord of the Face of the Sun.
Central America, Mexican, Yucatec Mayan	Ix U Sihnal	Moon goddess of health, healing, procreation, childbirth, water, and the curing of ulcers.
	Ixtab	Goddess of medicine, health, healing, justice, water, the moon, homes, weaving, rainbow, heaven and hell, and those who die in childbirth, battle, or due to suicide.
Central America, Mexico, Aztec	Teteoinnan, Teteoninnan	Goddess of healers, midwives, nature, the Earth, and fertility. Called The Mother of Sacred Ones.
	Tlazolteotl	Goddess of sexuality, purification, midwives, healers,

Appendix B

CULTURE	NAME	DESCRIPTION
		weavers, household affairs, immortality, magick, and time. The "Filth Goddess," who takes on herself the sins of those confessing to her.
	Tzapotla Tenan, Tzaputaltena	Goddess of herbal healing, treating skin diseases, and sore throats.
Central America, Mexico, Seri	Ahnt Kai'	Goddess of health, healing, education, knowledge, arts, ceremonies; mother and guardian.
Europe and Asia, Slavic, Russia	Mati Syra Zemlya	Featured
Europe and Asia, Slavic, Siberia, Trans-Baikal Buriat	Almoshi	Goddess of health and healing, especially domesticated animals, particularly cattle.
Europe and Asia, Slavic, Siberia, Yakut	Ajysit	Goddess of birth, fate, nursing, ceremonies, heaven and hell. Called The Milk Lake Mother.
Europe and Asia, Slavic, Siberia, Yakut	Nalygyr-aissyt-khotun	Benevolent goddess of childbirth, the sky, and the heavens.
Europe and Asia, Slavic, Siberia, Yukaghir	Numod-emei	Goddess of the home, health, and healing.
Europe and Mediterranean, Celtic and Roman especially in the Rhineland.	Hooded Spirits, Genii Cucullati	Spirits associated with health and fertility, and who sometimes carry egg-shapes and swords, perhaps symbolizing life, death, and rebirth.
Europe, Basque	Akerbeltz	Goddess of healing, health, protection from disease, beauty, charity, peace, harvest, and thankfulness. Symbols: rainbows and healing amulets.
Europe, Britain, Gaul, also Rome	Maponus, Maponos, Apollo Maponus, Mabon	God of healing and springs, poetry, song, and youthful beauty. Name means Young Boy, and Son, or Great Son.
Europe, Celtic	Alauna	A river goddess associated with healing; see Alaunus.

Region and Culture

CULTURE	NAME	DESCRIPTION
	Alaunus	God of healing prophecy, and the sun; see Alauna.
Europe, Celtic	Aveta	Water goddess who had a healing spring at Trier in Germany, and was shown as a nursing mother.
Europe, Celtic	Bel, Belenus, Belinos, Beli Mawr	Great god of sun, fire, purification, fertility, healing, prosperity, cattle, and more. Name means Shining.
	Epona	Goddess of horses, fertility, maternity, healing springs, sovereignty, prosperity, dogs, and more. Name means The Great Mare.
	Habondia, Habonde	Witchy goddess of abundance, fertility, cleansing, health, joy, luck, and magick. Dance around her ritual fire and let its smoke cleanse you. Symbols: ale and fires.
	Ianuaria	Goddess revered at a sacred spring and shrine in Burgundy. Shown as a young girl with curly hair, holding pan-pipes, and wearing a pleated coat. May be a healing goddess, or a music goddess, or both, since music can help heal.
	Miach	Son of DIAN CECHT. Brilliant surgeon. 365 different healing herbs grew on his grave.
	Rosmerta	Goddess of prosperity, sacred springs, healing shrines, trade, and abundance. Carries a bag of food or a basket of fruit.
	Sequana	River goddess of good health, luck, youthfulness, and movement. Stands in a duck-shaped boat. Associated with April showers.

217

Appendix B

CULTURE	NAME	DESCRIPTION
Europe, Celtic	Sulis, Sul, Sulivia, Sel, Sullis	Goddess of sacred wells and springs, water, healing, eye health and vision, blessings, and community. Also a sun goddess with ever-burning fires in her temples. Shown wearing a heavy black cloak and a bearskin hat. Symbols: water, fire, bears, owls, and wheat cakes.
Europe, Celtic, Gaul	Grannus	Featured
	Mullo, Mars Mullo	God who specializes in healing diseases of the eye, though he heals other organs as well. Had many shrines and temples, and urban sanctuaries. Name means Mule.
Europe, Celtic, Gaul, Germany	Sirona	Featured
Europe, Celtic, Ireland	Aibheaog, Aibheaeg	Fire goddess whose sacred well held waters that could cure toothache, if the supplicant left a white stone.
	Airmed	Featured
	Bebhionn	Giant supernatural woman from the Isle of Women off the Irish west coast. She commanded all powers of healing, and traveled with magickal birds.
	Ceacht	Goddess of medicine. Name means Lesson.
	Caolainn	Goddess who ruled a healing well, and could cure any ailment of the eyes. Is a form of the Cailleach.
	Dian Cécht	Featured
Europe, Celtic, Ireland to Austria	Brigit	Featured
Europe, Celtic, Lusitanian (ancient people of the western Iberian Peninsula)	Borvo	Featured

218

CULTURE	NAME	DESCRIPTION
Europe, Celtic, Netherlands, Germany	Nehalennia	Featured
Europe, England	Coventina	River goddess of a sacred well in Northumberland, and goddess of healing, inspiration, and prophecy.
	Damara	Goddess of fertility, well-being, health, kindness, abundance, and luck. Associated with the month of May. Symbols: flowers and greenery.
	Habetrot	Goddess of spinning, healing, and magickal protective garments.
Europe, Finnish	Rauni, Maan-Eno, Ravdna, Roonikka	Forest Mother and goddess of thunder, the mountain ash, childbirth, and ease from pain.
Europe, Finno-Ugric, Baltic Finn	Haltia, Holdja	Goddess of the home, health, healing, the directions, luck, and domesticated animals.
Europe, Finno-Ugric, Erya, Moksha, Mordvin	Mastor-ava, Azer-ava	Earth mother goddess of healing, health, agriculture, and the harvest.
Europe, Finno-Ugric, Finland, Saami	Suonetar	Goddess of health and healing, and especially the veins, immortality, and magick.
Europe, Finno-Ugric, Lapland, Saami	Sarakka	Goddess of childbirth and the home, the hearth, spinning, hunting, and wild animals.
Europe, Gaul	Damona	Goddess who protects pets and domestic animals, and preserves their health.
Europe, Germanic	Buschgrossmutter	The queen of the Buschfrauen, elves with mossy feet, who lived in hollow trees in virgin forests, and knew all the secrets of herbs and healing. Name means The Grandmother of the Bushes.
	Hexe	Goddess of health, healing herbs, magick charms, banishing

Appendix B

CULTURE	NAME	DESCRIPTION
		curses, and teaching spells and charms. A favorite of German Witches.
Europe, Germanic	The Wilden Wip	Female forest spirits of healing, magick, and sexuality; they like human men.
Europe, Lusitania (western Iberian Peninsula)	Endovelicus	Featured
Europe, Mediterranean, Gauls, Romans	Atepomarus, Apollo Atepomarus	Healing god sometimes called Apollo Atepomarus. His name means Great Horseman, or Owner of a Great Horse.
Europe, Norse and Teutonic	Gefn	Joyous goddess of the sun, spring, health, fertility, love, abundance, divination, and growth. Name means Giver. Symbols: all green and growing things.
Europe, Romano-Celtic, Britain	Nodens	Featured
Europe, Scandinavia, Finno Ugric, Sami	Maddarakka	Goddess of healing, caring for the spirits of the unborn, and childbirth. Called Old Woman.
Europe, Slavic	Dziwozony, Divozenky, Divi-Te-Zeni	The Wild Women of the Woods, who lived in burrows, and knew the secrets of herbal medicine. Shown as red and square-headed, with long fingers.
	Khors	God of health and hunting. Appears as a stallion.
	Mokosh	Goddess of spinning, rain, abundance, health, and the healing of the handicapped. Symbols: breast-shaped stones.
	Perun, Pyerun, Piorun, Peron, Perunu, Perkaunas	Supreme creator god of thunder and lightning, purification, fertility, defense against illness, and much more. Name means Thunder.

220

Region and Culture

CULTURE	NAME	DESCRIPTION
Europe, Slavic	Ved'ma	Goddess of magick, witchcraft, medicinal plants, rain and storms. Keeper of the sacred water of life and death.
	Zarya	Goddess of the healing waters, such as sacred springs and holy wells.
	Ziva, Siva, Zywie	Goddess of life, health, healing, longevity, regeneration, and rebirth. Her name means Living.
Europe, Slavic, Albania	The Perit	Mountain spirits of health, healing, earth, nature, time, and justice. They dress all in white.
Europe, Slavic, Bulgarian, Serbian, and Russian	Kupalo/Kupala	Featured
Europe, Slavic, Latvia, Lithuania, Prussia	Piluitus, Pilnitis, Pilwittus	Goddess or possibly god, of healing, fertility, agriculture, and the harvest.
Europe, Slavic, Russia, Cheremis	Purt-kūva	Goddess of the household, fate, luck, healing, and wealth. Name means House Woman. She is temperamental if not given offerings of beer and bread.
Europe, Slavic, Russia, Mordvin	Nastasija	Goddess of sleep, health, and healing.
Europe, Slavic, Serbia, Slovenia	The Vila, Willi, Judy, Samovila	Shape-shifting forest spirits of nature, earth, healing, agriculture, knowledge, wealth, justice, and ceremonies.
Europe, Slavic, Siberia, Yukaghir	Yegiled-emei	Fire goddess of healing.
Europe, Swiss	Lada	Goddess who sweeps away illness with her skirts, and ushers in the spring. Goddess of protection, kinship, energy, and joy. Symbols: birch tree, bells.
Europe, Teutonic	Gunnloed	Goddess of health, fertility, protection, wisdom, poetry, and creativity. Giantess who holds a cup of mead. Symbols: apples, and cauldron or cup.

Appendix B

CULTURE	NAME	DESCRIPTION
Europe, Teutonic	Hertha	Goddess of fertility, health, longevity, rebirth, tradition, nature, and domesticated animals. She descends through the smoke of a fire and brings gifts. Symbols: dormant trees and snow.
	Nerthus	Earth goddess of health, spring, energy, peace, and prosperity. Symbols: fire, chariot, and soil.
Europe/Mediterannean, Gaul, Rome	Glanis (Celtic), Valetudo (Roman)	God associated with a healing spring where pilgrims bathed, in southern France.
	Iovantucarus	God of healing who protected of youth in particular. Associated with Lenus Mars and also Mercury. Liked pet birds as offerings.
Europe/Mediterannean, Gaul, Rome, Greece	Lenus, Lenus Mars, Ocelus Vellaunus	Healing and protective god is depicted as a warrior with a Corinthian-style helmet. His sanctuaries included temples, shrines, baths, sleeping rooms for pilgrims, and even theaters. Worked with the goddesses Ancamna Victoria and Inciona.
Europe/Asia, Slavic, Siberia	Mamaldi	Creator goddess of health, healing, and magick.
India and Persia, Hindu	Soma, Amrit, Amrita, Chandra, Haoma, Indu, and others	Healing god connected with soma, the drink of the gods. God of herbs, flowing waters, inspiration, wealth, and the moon. Shown as a celestial bull, a youth, or a bird. His symbol is the silver crescent.
India, Bengali	Janguli	Golden snake goddess with six hands, who can heal snakebite.
India, Buddhist	Shimhanada, Lokeswara	An aspect of Avalokitesvara; he is healer of all diseases. Wears a tiger skin, sits on a lion, and holds a trident with a white snake wrapped around it.

Region and Culture

CULTURE	NAME	DESCRIPTION
India, Hindu	Ashvins, Ashwini, Dasra and Nasatya	Divine twins, physicians of the gods and patrons of Ayurvedic medicine. Shown as twin horsemen, or both in a golden chariot, sometimes as men with horses' heads.
	Dhanvantari	Featured
	Dhatri	Solar deity and god of health and domestic tranquility. Name means Earth. Can be invoked by drawing sacred diagrams and chanting certain hymns.
	Ganga	Goddess of the river Ganges, and purifications, cleansing, health, wellness, and mercy. Stands on a sea monster. Symbols: water, yellow things.
	Māri, Mariamman, Maariamma, Mariaai, Amman, Aatha	South Indian mother goddess, and deity of disease and rain. Associated with the goddesses Parvati, Durga, and Shitaladevi, and may be an aspect of Kali. Heals diseases like chicken pox, smallpox, and cholera.
	Nirriti	Old woman goddess, who takes on the burdens of the world, including disease. Dresses all in black. Patron of the poor as long as they attempt to live a good life.
	Savitri	Goddess of healing, long life, immortality, sunrise, sunset, night, and rest. Shown as golden-haired goddess in a chariot drawn by two bright horses.
	Tamra	The ancestress of all birds and goddess of health, longevity, relationships, devotion, nature, earth, air, and communications from the gods. Symbols: feathers and birdseed.

Appendix B

CULTURE	NAME	DESCRIPTION
India, Hindu	Vaidya-Nath	A healing aspect of Shiva; Lord of the Knowing Ones, or Lord of the Physicians.
India, Tibet, Buddhist, Hindu	Yamantaka, Manjusri and more	God, Destroyer of Death, shown with the head of a bull, a third eye, wearing a crown of skulls.
India/Buddhist the master session	Bhaishajyaguru, Bhaisajyaguru, Man-La, Sang-Gyeman-Gyila-Bduryr-O-Chi-Gyal-Po (Tibet), Yao-Shih Fu (China)	God of healing and sex change, master physician, God of healing and spells. Shown as blue. Rules the east, and holds fruit in his right hand.
Indian Ocean, Sri Lanka	Kiri Amma	Seven-fold goddess who heals diseases in children, and blesses nursing mothers. Name can mean Grandmother, Milk Mother, or Wet Nurse.
Mediterannean, Greek	Paean, Paeëon, Paieon, Paeon, Paion	Wise physician of the gods, who knows the remedies for all illnesses, and brings healing and relief from pain.
Mediterannean, Roman	Vejovis	Featured
	Verminus	God who protects cattle from disease.
Mediterranean, Dacian or Thracian	Derzelas, Darzalas	God of health and the vitality of the human spirit, as well as abundance and the underworld. Shown holding cornucopiae. Sacred games were held every five years to honor him.
Mediterranean, Etruscan	Fufluns	Featured
	Menrva	Featured
Mediterranean, Greek	Agathos Diamon, Agathadeamon, Agthodiamon	Deity of good fortune, health, and life.
	Asclepius	Featured
	Chiron	Featured
	Damia	Goddess of health, especially women's health; worshipped only by women.

… Region and Culture

CULTURE	NAME	DESCRIPTION
	Herakles	Featured
Mediterranean, Greek, Cretan	Eileithyia	Featured
Mediterranean, Greek, Roman	Apollo	Featured
	Artemis/Diana	Featured
	Hygieia	Featured
Mediterranean, Phoenicia	Shadrapha, Shadrafa, Shed the Healer	God of healing, and conqueror of evil. He stands on a lion, under a sun symbol.
Mediterranean, Phoenicia and others	Eshmun	Featured
Mediterranean, Roman	Angitia	Featured
	Anna Parenna	Goddess of cycles, grounding, kindness, longevity, and peace. Name means Enduring Year. Symbols: wine and circles (wheels, rings, wreaths).
	Bona Dea	Featured
	Carmentis, Carmenta, Nicostrata, Postverta	Goddess of birth, children, fertility, healing, prophecy. Name means a spell or charm in the form of a song. Symbols: music and babies.
	Carna	Featured
	Cura	The Goddess who created humans from clay, and provides cures for all diseases.
	Cybele	Goddess of health, strength, love, relationships, victory, and humor. Symbols: meteorite or black stone, pine tree, and key.
	Febris	Goddess who could cause or cure malaria and fevers. Said be be an honest and shrewd deity.
	Fons	Goddess of fountains, springs, fresh drinking water, healing, and thankfulness. The cleansing and healing power of clean water.

Appendix B

CULTURE	NAME	DESCRIPTION
Mediterranean, Roman	Juturna	Goddess of healing springs; bathing in her fountain healed and renewed health.
	Medica, Minerva Medica	The goddess Minerva in her role as the patroness of physicians.
	Meditrina	Goddess of health, healing magick and charms, herbal preparations, and wine.
	Orbona	Goddess of healing and safety for children.
	Phoebus	Roman equivalent of Apollo, god of medicine, the healing rays of the sun, and protection against plague.
	Salus	Goddess of health, public welfare, and prosperity.
	Vejovis	Featured
	Verminus	God who protects cattle from disease.
Mesopotamia	Nina	Mother goddess of herbal healing, health, herb magick, mediation, dreams, cooperation, magick, and civilization. Protects well-being over the winter.
	Ningishzida	God (though sometimes said to be female) of medicine and the underworld. Name means Lord of the Good Tree. Occasionally shown as a serpent with a human head. Associated with Ningishzida is the earliest known symbol of snakes twining around a rod or staff, predating the Rod of Asclepius and the Caduceus of Hermes by more than thousand years.
	Ninurta, Ningirsu, Ninib, Ninip	God of healing, hunting and war, and the South Wind. Battles monsters and carries a sword, mace, or bow and arrows.

CULTURE	NAME	DESCRIPTION
Mesopotamia, Babylonia, Sumer	Ninsu-Utud, Ninsutu	Goddess of healing, especially aching teeth. One of the deities born to relieve the illness of Enki.
Mesopotamia, Phoenicia	Aherah	Goddess of birth, blessings, health, divination, law, luck, carpentry, masonry, and wisdom. The Mother of All Wisdom, Proprietress of Universal Law. Symbols: brick and a wooden pole.
Mesopotamia, Sumerian	Nanna, Nina	Goddess of herbs, healing, magickm, the moon, dreams, and civilization. Called The Holy One of Many Names.
	Ninazu	Benevolent god of healing and the underworld. The consort of **Ninsutu**, one of the deities born to relieve the illness of Enki. The patron deity of the city of Eshnunna.
	Ninti	One of eight goddesses of healing created by NINHURSAG; specializing in the ribs.
	Nintil	One of eight goddesses of healing created by NINHURSAG.
	Nintud, Innini, Ninanna, Nintu, Belit, Belit-Ilani	Mother earth goddess of childbirth
	Ninhursag	Featured
Mesopotamia, Sumerian, Babylonian, Assyrian, Akkadian	Gula	Featured
Mesopotamia	Namtar, Namtaru, Namtara	Minor god of death and disease, and the messenger of An, Ereshkigal, and Nergal. Name means Destiny, or Fate.
Mesopotamia/ Anatolia, Hurrian and Hittite	Shaushka	Featured

227

Appendix B

CULTURE	NAME	DESCRIPTION
Middle East, Arab	Salema and Sakia	Gods of health and rain, respectively.
Middle East, Hittite	Kamrusepas, Kamrusepa	Goddess of healing, medicine, magick, chanting, ritual purification, and spells. Can remove or redirect the anger of gods and men, so that it is harmless.
Middle East, Persia	Ahurani	Goddess of fertility, growth, harvest, health, insight, longevity, luck, and prosperity. Symbols: water and beverages.
	Three-Legged Ass	Benevolent god who destroys disease and pests. As large as a mountain, with three giant feet, six eyes, and nine mouths.
	Thrita, Faridun, Thraetana and more	Healing god who drives away serious disease and death. Patron of healing plants, and relieves itches, fevers, and incontinence.
Middle East, Persia, Zoroastrian	Haoma	God of health, healing, and fertility named for a divine plant, the King of Herbs, thought to be ephedra. Associated with purification and the continuity of life—even including immortality; and is patron of the priesthood.
Middle East, Persia, Zoroastrian	Haurvatat, Ameretat, Khurdad, Amardad	Goddesses of health and immortality, water, vegetation, and wealth.
North America, Arctic, Baffin Land Inuit	Kattakju	Goddess of healing, who helps shamans in their work with those who are ill.
North America, Arctic, Baffin Land Inuit	Sinnilktok	Very benevolent goddess of health, healing, domesticated animals, food, who appears as a creature who is half human and half dog.

Region and Culture

CULTURE	NAME	DESCRIPTION
North America, Arctic, Caribou Inuit	Pinga	Goddess of fertility, medicine, reincarnation, and the hunt. Also guided the souls of the dead to the underworld. Guardian of animals. Name means The One Who is [Up On] High.
North America, Arctic, Iglulik Inuit	Takanakapsaluk	Arctic sea goddess of personal health, healing, purification, strength, thankfulness, luck, hunting, wild animals, justice and judgment, and caring for the spirits of the dead.
North America, California, Chumash	'Alahtin	Moon goddess of cleansing and purification, health, healing, prosperity, the calendar, the tides, and menstrual periods.
	Momoy	Goddess of ancestors, shamans, immortality, healing, magick, knowledge, widows and foster parents, adoption, social rules, and tradition.
North America, Hopi	Angak	A kachina spirit of healing and rain, shown with long, black hair, holding an evergreen branch and with raincloud symbols on his costume.
North America, Inuit	Eeyeekalduk	God of healing medicine and good health. Shown as a small man with a black face, lives in a small stone. He drew illness from the patient into himself, through his eyes, and could also send illness from himself to to others through his eyes.
North America, Iroquois	Hadui	God of disease, medicine, and cures, seen as a hunchbacked dwarf.
North America, Native American	Mother Of All Eagles	Represents health, healing, power, destiny, freedom, perspective, vision, air, and movement. Symbols: feathers.

229

Appendix B

CULTURE	NAME	DESCRIPTION
North America, Native American	Unkatahe	Water deity, depicted as a sacred serpent. He or she has power over disease and the transmigration of souls, and is shown with crescent horns representing the moon, as well as circles and spiral designs.
North America, Navajo	Glispa	Goddess of magick, ceremonies, health, healing, knowledge, sand painting, and feather offerings. Brought the healing chant, Hozoni, to the people. May have been a form of the goddess Estsanatlehi, or Turquoise Woman.
North America, Northeast, Lenape	No'oma Cawaneyung	Goddess of healing, medicinal plants, and the directions. Grandmother of the South.
North America, Northeast, Penobscot	Pakwaekasiasit	Goddess of medicinal herbs. Arrow-head Finger.
North America, Northeast, Seneca	Onenha	Corn goddess of healing, agriculture, knowledge, and the Corn Harvest Ceremony.
North America, Northwest, Bella Coola	Aialila'axa	Goddess of the moon and night, and healing, who protects from illness and death.
	L'etsa'aplelana	Goddess of magick, ceremonies, healing, and the initiation of medicine people.
	Tlitcaplitana	Goddess of the sky, the heavens, healing, knowledge, and magick. Descended from the heavens, to share health, healing, and the secret knowledge and chants. She could sing people to health with her beautiful voice, though not physically attractive—she had a big nose.

CULTURE	NAME	DESCRIPTION
North America, Pacific Northwest, Nuxalk and Kwakwaka'wakw Nations	Kumugwe	Featured
North America, Plains, Arikara, Pawnee, Cheyenne, Mandan, Hidatsa	Corn Mother, Mother Sunset Yellow	The maize plant personified as a goddess of health, healing, agriculture, fertility, knowledge, ceremonies, and medicine bundles.
North America, Plains, Crow	Miritatsiec	Moon goddess of the night, healing, hunting, and wild animals, who teaches the healing arts and aids those who are suffering or lost.
North America, Plains, Kiowa	Pasowee, Buffalo Old Woman	Buffalo Woman, goddess of health, healing, medicine, knowledge, hunting, wild animals, and home and shelter.
North America, Plains, Pawnee	Big Black Meteor Star	Goddess of stars, planets, healing, and knowledge. Called Star of Magic; teaches medicine people their craft.
	Red-spider-woman	Goddess of healing, insects, and farming, especially beans, squash, and corn—the "three sisters" of southwest farming.
North America, Pueblo	Mina Koya	Goddess of salt, cleansing, protecting, preserving, health, healing power, blessing, and weather. Symbol: salt. Celebrated in the autumn.
North America, Southeast, Cherokee	Nundã	Goddess of the sun, the day, healing, time, calendars, and death. She can cause fevers and headaches, and heal them.
North America, Southwest, Cochiti and other Pueblo Nations	Uretsete and Naotste	Featured

Appendix B

CULTURE	NAME	DESCRIPTION
North America, Southwest, Pueblo	Badger Old Woman	Goddess of childbirth, hunting, wild animals, ceremonies, and the gateway to the other world of the kachinas.
North America, Southwest, Yavapai	Komwidapokuwia	Creator goddess of life, magick, healing, and protection for healers.
	Widapokwi	Goddess of health, healing, medicine songs, and protection from storms and whirlwinds.
North America, Southwest, Zuni	Yanauluha	God of healing, agriculture, animal husbandry, knowledge, and civilization. The Great Medicine Man.
	Tcakwena Okya	Goddess or kachina of fertility, childbirth, protection of children, and longevity.
Northern Europe; Sámi	Beiwe	Featured
Oceania, Polynesia, Hawaii, New Zealand	Haumea	Featured
Pacific, Polynesia, Hawaii	Hi'iaka I ka pua'ena'ena, Hiata ta bu enaena,	Goddess of healing, leis, and kava—the drink of the gods, travel and trade. As a healer, she is named Kuku 'ena I kea hi ho'omau honua. Pele's sister.
Pacific, Polynesia, Hawaii	Hina lau limu kala	Sea goddess of health, healing, medicines from the sea, and ceremonies.
	Kāne kua'ana	Human woman who transformed into a dragon or lizard goddess of health, healing, fishing, abundance, reptiles, and creatures of the sea. Honor her with a fire altar, and she will protect you from sickness and bring you wealth.
	Kapo	Goddess of childbirth, and termination of pregnancy.
	Uli, Ouli	Goddess of life, death, healing, magick, and curses.

CULTURE	NAME	DESCRIPTION
Pacific, Polynesia, Hawaii, New Zealand, Maori	Hina uri	Goddess of the night, dark moon, and childbirth. She is Māui's sister.
Pacific, Polynesia, Marquesas Islands	Niniano	Goddess of healing, fishing, water creatures, family, tribe, and community.
Pacific, Polynesia, New Zealand, Maori	Rua hine metua	Goddess of protection, joy, inner peace, emotional healing, and order. Called Old Mother.
Pacific, Polynesia, Raiatea	Te vahine nui tahu ra'i	Goddess of healing after serious sickness, protection, fire, fire-walkers, and magick.
Pacific, Polynesia, Tahiti	Hina tahu tahu	Goddess of healing, divination, and fate.
Pacific, Polynesia, Tahiti, Society Islands (Ta'aroa)	Ai tūpua'i	Goddess of war, health, and healing.
Polynesian	Ha'iaka	Goddess of healing, flowers, and magick. Born in the shape of an egg.
	Waiora, Waiola, Vai-Ola	Goddess of health, who had a sacred well that could cure all disease. Name means Water of Life.
Scandanavia, Vanir	Gulliveig	Goddess of magick, healing, and prophesy. Name means Golden Branch.
Scandinavia, Norse, Teutonic	Eir	Featured
Siberia, Yukut	Itchita	Birch tree goddess of healing and protection; spirits of grass and trees are her tiny helpers.
South America, Brazil, Belem	Senhora Ana	Goddess of health, healing, the elderly, altruism, and humility.
South America, Brazil, Ita	Apolonia, Saint	Goddess or saint of healing, especially for toothache or other dental problems.
South America, Ecuador	Umina	God of medicine, represented by a large emerald.
South America, Inca	Imaymana Viracocha	God who tells mortals of the healing properties of plants, and warns of dangerous ones.

233

Appendix B

CULTURE	NAME	DESCRIPTION
South America, Peru	Cocamama	Goddess of healing, health, happiness, love, sexuality, the Earth, nature, selfishness, life and death. Mother of the coca plant.
South America, Peru, Huarochiri	Mirahuato	Goddess of health and healing.
South America, Peru, Inca, Chincha	Mama Cocha	Featured
Southeast Asia, Burma, Katchins	Katsin Numka Majan	Goddess of healing, especially the lungs, heart, liver, and other internal organs. Called the Mother of Vital Organs.
Southeast Asia, Cambodia	Po Yan Dari	Goddess of death and disease, but also health and healing; can be found in caves—leave offerings there.
Southeast Asia, Philippines, Apayao	Dinawagan	Goddess of health and healing.
Southeast Asia, Philippines, Bukidnon	Ibabasag	Goddess of pregnancy and childbirth.
	Panglang	Goddess of unborn children, pregnancy, and childbirth. Patron of midwives.
Southeast Asia, Vietnam, Chams	Pajau Yan	Featured
Tibet, Buddhist	Medicine Buddhas, Abheda, Mi-Che-Pa, Mi-P'yed	Appear in groups of eight or nine, wearing monks' robes, and are said to have supernatural wisdom.

Appendix C
Healing Modalities

Our bodies are remarkably capable of healing themselves, but sometimes an intervention is required. If you are seriously ill or injured, we hope that you have already enlisted the services of a professional healer, or will consider doing so. Often "alternative" therapies like acupuncture or homeopathy can complement the methods of allopathic (Western) medicine. We offer this list as a reference if you are considering initial treatment, or adding another modality. Best wishes with whatever you choose.

ACUPRESSURE	
	Use of deep pressure on the energy meridians, to balance the energy flow of the chi/qi and thereby promote healing. Similar to acupuncture, but uses pressure instead of needles. Originated in China.
ACUPUNCTURE	
	Use of needles on the energy meridians, to balance the energy flow of the chi/qi and thereby promote healing. Originated in China.
AFFIRMATIONS	
	Use of many repetitions of positive statements (I am happy and healthy) to reprogram the mind into believing the statement is true.
AFFORMATIONS	
	Developed by Noah St. John, the use of positive questions that assume the desired state, in order to enlist the aid of the unconscious and subconscious in finding the answers, thereby improving mental or physical health. For instance, How is it that I am consistently healthy and happy?

ALLOPATHIC MEDICINE	
	"Standard" medicine, using diagnosis of an ailment, the use of drugs, nutrition, and surgery to "correct" the ailment.
AROMATHERAPY	
	Use of various scents to calm or change mental or physical health.
ART THERAPY	
	Use of art techniques (painting, drawing, sculpting, etc.) to improve mental and physical health.
AYURVEDIC MEDICINE	
	Ancient Indian system of nutrition and energy work designed to align the body with its fundamental energy.
BIOFEEDBACK	
	Use of a biofeedback machine, which measures breathing rate, heart rate, and blood pressure, to become aware of the body's unconscious reactions to stimuli, and then practices to bring those reactions under conscious control.
BREATH THERAPY	
	Using breathing techniques, many based in Prana (breath) Yoga, to clear the energy of the body and promote healing and total presence in the moment.
CHEMOTHERAPY	
	Primarily used to treat cancer, uses chemicals to destroy the malignant cells. Has many side effects, so should be used only under medical supervision.
CHINESE MEDICINE	
	Use of intense observation of the client for diagnosis, then use of acupuncture, herbs, medicines, and energy work for healing.
CHIROPRACTIC	
	Use of body manipulation to realign the body, especially the spinal column, misalignment of which is held to cause other disorders.
COLOR THERAPY	
	Use of colors, both light and fabrics or paints, to influence the emotions and physical health. For instance, yellow is a calm, cheering color that influences the solar plexus chakra, bringing heightened self-responsibility.
CRANIOSACRAL THERAPY	
	Massage and manipulation of the bones of the head and shoulders, and the muscles over them, to promote relaxation, realignment, and healing of emotional and physical issues.
CRYSTALS AND STONES	
	Use of various crystals and stones, thought to have specific healing properties. For instance, carnelian is good for blood or energy issues, and for deep comfort and relaxation.

DANCE THERAPY	
	Use of dance and movement to promote physical and emotional healing.
DREAMWORK	
	Analyzing dreams to find clues to emotional, spiritual, and sometimes physical issues. Also setting the intention to experience "lucid dreaming," or dreaming directed by the conscious mind.
ENERGY HEALING (Includes REIKI, THERAPEUTIC TOUCH, etc.)	
	"Running energy" through the practitioner's hands, to the client's body to promote health.
FLOWER ESSENCES (Bach)	
	Use of a dilute quantity of flowers in water; used for mental and emotional healing, and sometimes physical healing.
HERBALISM/HERBAL THERAPY	
	Use of medicinal herbs to stimulate and heal the physical body.
HOMEOPATHY	
	Based on the premise that "like cures like," users believe that minute quantities of what caused an illness can be used to cure it.
HYDROTHERAPY aka BALNEOTHERAPY, WATSU (water)	
	Movement in water designed to improve mental or physical health.
HYPNOSIS	
	An induced trance-like state, used to create suggestions for improved mental or physical health, or re-alignment of deeply held beliefs.
LIGHT	
	Use of different light wavelengths and colors to improve mental and physical health. For instance, the use of bright, cool light to treat Seasonal Affective Disorder.
MAGNET THERAPY	
	Use of magnets on various parts of the body to realign the magnetic field.
MASSAGE (Includes ROLFING, SHIATSU, etc.)	
	Use of the hands, fingers, elbows, (and some tools) to apply light to heavy pressure and movement on muscles. Used for relaxation, and, in the cases of deep-tissue massage, like Rolfing, to realign the body.
MEDITATION	
	Diverse methods used to quiet and focus (or unfocus) the mind, creating a relaxed awareness.
MOVEMENT EDUCATION (Feldenkreis, Alexander Technique, etc.)	
	Detailed, specific movements designed to re-educate the body into proper movement patterns for physical and mental health.
MUSIC AND SOUND THERAPY	
	Use of sounds, music, tones, harmonies for healing. Aligns and balances the right and left hemispheres of the brain, and promotes

	relaxation, improves memory, and creates mind/body connection and spatial and temporal awareness.
NATUROPATHY (combines others)	
	Using, or becoming aligned with, the vital force or healing force of nature, the *irs medicatrix naturae*.
NUTRITIONAL HEALING	
	Use of food as a means of balancing and rejuvenating the body.
OSTEOPATHY	
	Use of physical manipulation to realign the body. Also uses nutrition, psychotherapy, medicines, and surgery when needed.
PSYCHOTHERAPY	
	Use of talk, role-playing, and other means to bring emotional balance.
QI/CHI: QIGONG, TAI CHI, etc.	
	Use of stylized movements to enhance the flow of chi/qi through the body to enhance health and well-being.
RADIATION	
	Used primarily for the treatment of cancer. It has side effects, and requires medical supervision.
REFLEXOLOGY	
	Massage and acupressure on the feet, working points that correspond to other systems in the body. Moves chi/qi to improve health.
RELAXATION THERAPY	
	Use of breathing, biofeedback, muscle tension/relaxation techniques to calm the body and mind and enhance healing.
SHAMANIC HEALING	
	Use of rhythmic drumming, chanting, and other techniques to encourage the body or mind to heal.
SURGERY	
	Using surgical tools and techniques to cut into the body to remove illness or correct injury, and allow healing.
VISUALIZATION	
	Use of guided imagery (including visual, auditory, kinesthetic modes), to achieve a trance-like state or to imagine the body, mind, or circumstances changed.
VITAMIN AND MINERAL THERAPY	
	Using (often) large doses of specific vitamins or minerals to rebalance the body. For instance, the use of megadoses of Vitamin D2 to increase D in the body.
YOGA	
	Use of specific postures, stretches, breathing techniques, and visualization to align the body and mind and allow healing.

Appendix D
The Middle Pillar for Healing

The Middle Pillar is used to open, balance, and energize the chakras (energy centers of the human body). This version involves vibrating the names of healing deities. (To vibrate the names means to intone them loud, long, and with power.) You can call upon goddesses or gods (listed afterwards), or use a mix of both.

In this first version, name the following goddesses:

Crown: ISIS (Egyptian)

Third Eye: MENRVA (Etruscan)

Throat: AIRMED (Celtic)

Heart: CARNA (physical) (Roman) or KWAN YIN (compassion) (Asian)

Energy (solar plexus): BRIGIT (Celtic)

Sexual: ANAHITA (Persian)

Root: MATI SYRA ZEMLYA (Slavic)

1. Wear loose, comfortable clothing, or go skyclad.
2. Find a quiet place where you will not be disturbed.
3. Stand and breathe deeply into your abdomen.
4. Visualize a glowing ball of energy at the top of your head (CROWN CHAKRA). Vibrate the Name ISIS.

5. Follow the channel of energy down to the middle of your forehead, and visualize a glowing ball of energy there (THIRD EYE CHAKRA). Still holding the image of the first chakra, vibrate the Name MENRVA.

6. Follow the channel of energy down to your throat, and visualize a glowing ball of energy there (THROAT CHAKRA). Still holding the image of the first two chakras, vibrate the Name AIRMED.

7. Follow the channel of energy down to your heart, and visualize a glowing ball of energy there (HEART CHAKRA). Still holding the image of the first three chakras, vibrate the Name CARNA.

8. Follow the channel of energy down to your solar plexus, and visualize a glowing ball of energy there (ENERGY CHAKRA). Still holding the image of the first four chakras, vibrate the Name BRIGIT.

9. Follow the channel of energy down to a point above your genitals, and visualize a glowing ball of energy there (SEXUAL CHAKRA). Still holding the image of the first five chakras, vibrate the Name ANAHITA.

10. Follow the channel of energy down to the base of your spine, and visualize a glowing ball of energy there (ROOT CHAKRA). Still holding the image of the first six chakras, vibrate the Name MATI SYRA ZEMLYA.

11. Holding the image of all seven chakras, take three deep breaths. As you inhale, pull energy up along your back to your crown chakra. As you exhale, move your awareness down along your front to your root chakra.

12. Still holding the image of all seven chakras, take three deep

breaths. As you inhale, pull energy up along your left side to your crown chakra. As you exhale, move your awareness down along your right side to your root chakra.
13. Still holding the image of all seven chakras, take PAIRS of deep breaths: As you inhale, pull energy up to your energy chakra. As you exhale, hold the energy there. As you inhale again, bring the energy from there up through your crown chakra. As you exhale, let in pour down around the outside of your body. Do three sets like this.
14. Beginning at the bottoms of your feet and moving deosil, wrap yourself in a band of light, all the way up to your crown chakra: "tie it off" there. Take as many breaths as you need. Think of this wrapping as a semi-permeable membrane that holds in your energy, and allows light, life, love, and air to pass freely through in to you.
15. Rest in silence for a moment, sensing your energy field.

Healing gods:
Crown: EBISU (Japan)
Third Eye: ENDOVELICUS (Lusitania)
Throat: CHIRON (Greek)
Heart: NODENS (Celtic)
Energy (solar plexus): BORVO (Celtic)
Sexual: HERAKLES (Greek)
Root: VEJOVIS (Roman)

© Amber K, 4/1994 and Amber K and Azrael Arynn K 1/2018

Appendix E
Symbols

Words are symbols; pictures are symbols; glyphs and sigils and even logos are symbols. A symbol is "a thing that represents or stands for something else, such as a mark, character, shape or sign." Some symbols are thousands of years old, predating any alphabet, and have deep layers of meaning.

Symbols of power evoke feelings, ideas, and concepts in our minds, and can even change our biochemistry by triggering powerful emotions. You can take a healing symbol, reinforce its connection with the healing energies you want to tap, and create a talisman, pendant, altarpiece, or focal point for meditation, to boost the healing process.

In addition to the symbols we present here, you may find others to serve your purpose in the areas of alchemy, astrology, or mythology. You may find a symbol that connects with the particular deity you are working with, or one to enhance your health overall. Let us begin with some more general or widespread symbols, the Rod of Asclepius, and the Caduceus.

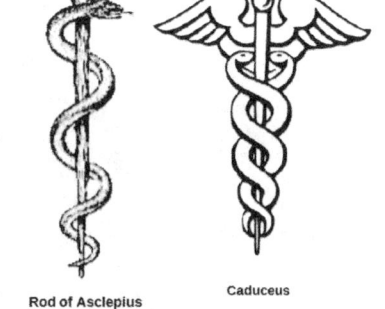

Appendix E

The rod of Asclepius, named for the mortal who became a god of healing, first appeared centuries earlier in Sumer. The Caduceus was originally known as the staff of Hermes, a Greek god of commerce, thieves, and sports. It mistakenly became associated with modern medicine at the beginning of the 20th century.

Now three more:

The Tree of Life and snakes have been associated with healing and regeneration for millennia, and the mortar and pestle has been adopted as a symbol of pharmacy.

Cho Ku Rei   Sei He Ki   Hon Sha Ze Sho Nen

Raku   Dai Ko Myo

Reiki is a Japanese (some say Chinese) method of energy healing. Certain symbols, primarily the ones shown at left, are used by reiki practitioners in their work.

It is probably best to avoid using these symbols unless you are trained by an experienced practitioner. However, anyone can learn reiki, although some teachers charge substantial fees for training.

The symbols below have been used by healers from various cultures around the world. L to R, top to bottom, they are:

shamanic sun, the reiki Antahkarana, the triskelion, the Zibu angelic symbol for healing hands, a Native American healing hand, one of many modern health and healing symbols from the fascinating website Sigil Athenaeum, Norse health bindrune, Voudun *Gran Bwa veve*.

Now on to more; many of the featured goddesses and gods are included here.

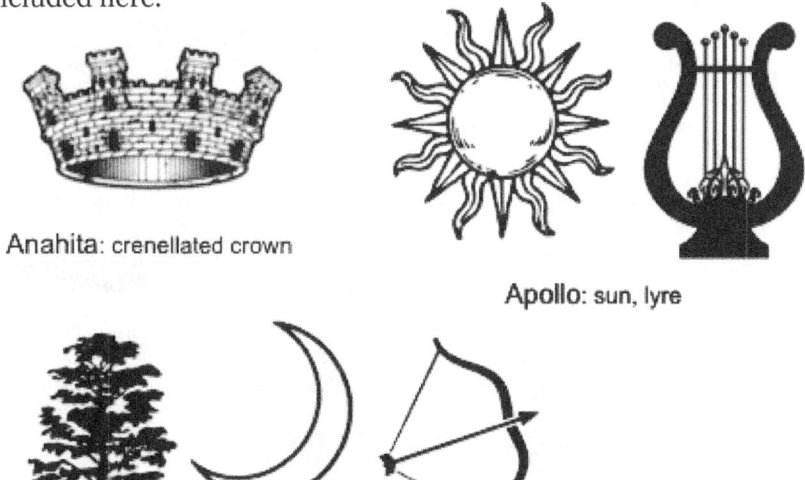

Anahita: crenellated crown

Apollo: sun, lyre

Artemis: cypress, crescent moon, bow and arrow

245

Appendix E

Babalu Aye: broom, pot with holes, cowrie shell

Brigit: Brigit's Cross

Bona Dea: serpent and cornucopia

Carna/Cardea: whitethorn twig

Dian Cécht: Silver hand

Ebisu: Large fish

Erinle: smooth river stone

Eileithyia: torch, white flowers

246

Symbols

Fufluns: thyrsus, grapes, wine cup

Heka: hieroglyph with raised arms, and a twist of flax

Gula: 8-rayed solar orb, Tree of Life, dog

Herakles: lionskin and club

Hygieia: bowl and entwined serpent

Ixchel: bowl, filled with rainwater or upturned and empty

Kumugwe: seal, octopus

Kupalo/Kupala: ferns, birch tree, flowers

247

Appendix E

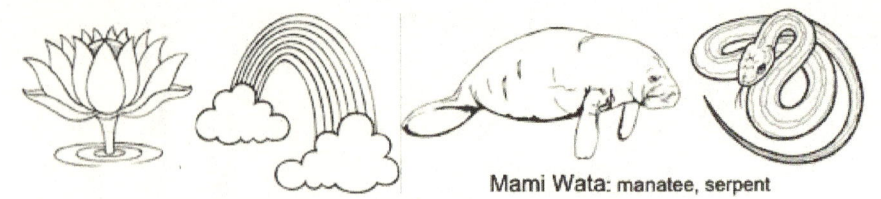

Kwan Yin: lotus, rainbow

Mami Wata: manatee, serpent

Menrva: lightning, owl, moon

Nehalennia: Ship, dog, basket of loaves and apples

Ninhursag: mountain, omega sign

Shaushka: lion, axe

Nodens: triton, dolphin, dog

Sekhmet: lioness, solar disc, uraeus

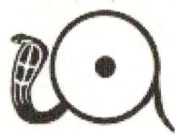

Symbols

Sitala: short broom, winnowing fan, jar of cooling water, or drinking cup

Vejovis: laurel wreath, arrow, lightning bolts

Tawaret: hippo with sun disc, sa hieroglyph

Sirona: paten, cornucopia, scepter, serpent, star, eggs

249

Appendix F
Reading List

Carlyon, Richard. *A Guide to the Gods*. William Morrow and Co., 1982.

Conway, D. J. *Magick of the Gods and Goddesses: How to Invoke Their Powers*. (Formerly *The Ancient and Shining Ones: World Myth, Magick and Religion*). Llewellyn, 1997.

Emerson, Ellen Russell. *Indian Myths: Or, Legends, Traditions, and Symbols of the Aborigines of North America Compared with Those of Other Countries, Including Hindostan, Egypt, Persia, Assyria, and China*. Public Domain. J. R. Osgood, 1884.

Evslin, Bernard. *Gods, Demigods, and Demons: An Encyclopedia of Greek Mythology*. Scholastic, Inc., 1975.

Fowler, Susan. *Why Motivating People Doesn't Work... and What Does*. Berrett-Koehler Publishers, 2017.

Imel, Martha Ann and Dorothy Myers. *Goddesses in World Mythology: A Biographical Dictionary*. Oxford University Press,

1993. Lists dozens of additional healing goddesses in the index. Most have a one-phrase or -sentence description.

The Internet: While the Internet can be a source for much good information, take what you read with a grain of salt, and make your own decisions, based on your own instincts.

Knappert, Jan. *Pacific Mythology: An Encyclopedia of Myth and Legend.* Aquarian/Thorsons, 1992.

Kravitz, David. *Who's Who in Greek and Roman Mythology.* Crown Pub, 1977.

Maslow, Abraham. *The Farther Reaches of Human Nature.* Viking, New York, 1971.

Monaghan, Patricia. *The New Book of Goddesses and Heroines.* Llewellyn, 1998.

Telesco, Patricia. *365 Goddess: A Daily Guide to the Magic and Inspiration of the Goddess.* HarperSanFrancisco, 1998.

Turner, Patricia, and Charles Russell Coulter. *Dictionary of Ancient Deities.* Oxford University Press, 2000.

Weil, Dr. Andrew. CD: *Breathing: The Master Key to Self-Healing.*

About the Authors

Between them, Amber and Azrael have been working with gods and goddesses for more than 65 years as Wiccan priestesses. With the aid of the goddesses and gods, and in conjunction with conventional and alternative healing modalities, they have met and overcome challenges of bipolar disorder, breast cancer, depression, diabetes, hypertension, leukemia, and osteoarthritis.

They have worked especially with Amaterasu, Artemis, Bast, Brigit, Coyote, Epona, Gaia, Ganesha, Hekate, Hygieia, Isis, Lakshmi, Nuit, and Persephone.

Both Amber and Azrael have extensive knowledge of and experience with world religions, and believe that all contain wisdom, and that each individual must discover their own path.

Both are Reiki practitioners. In addition, Azrael has made an extensive study of nutrition and its impact on health. Amber explores the healing energies of stones and crystals. They make their home in the high desert of New Mexico, at a non-profit educational and retreat center called Ardantane.

Made in the USA
Las Vegas, NV
25 May 2024